Laboratory Inquiry in Chemistry, Third Edition

ASU CHM 101 (and CHM 108 downtown)

Richard C. Bauer | James P. Birk | Douglas J. Sawyer

CENGAGE
Learning

Australia • Brazil • Japan • Korea • Mexico • Singapore • Spain • United Kingdom • United States

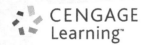

**Laboratory Inquiry in Chemistry, Third Edition:
ASU CHM 101 (and CHM 108 downtown)**

Richard C. Bauer | James P. Birk | Douglas J.
Sawyer

Executive Editors:
 Maureen Staudt
 Michael Stranz

Senior Project Development Manager:
 Linda DeStefano

Marketing Specialist:
 Sara Mercurio
 Lindsay Shapiro

Senior Production / Manufacturing Manager:
 Donna M. Brown

PreMedia Supervisor:
 Joel Brennecke

Rights & Permissions Specialist:
 Kalina Hintz
 Todd Osborne

Cover Image:
 Getty Images*

© 2009 Cengage Learning

For product information and technology assistance, contact us at
Cengage Learning Customer & Sales Support, 1-800-354-9706

For permission to use material from this text or product,
submit all requests online at **cengage.com/permissions**
Further permissions questions can be emailed to
permissionrequest@cengage.com

ISBN-13: 978-1-4240-8713-6

ISBN-10: 1-4240-8713-9

Cengage Learning
5191 Natorp Boulevard
Mason, Ohio 45040
USA

Cengage Learning is a leading provider of customized learning solutions with office locations around the globe, including Singapore, the United Kingdom, Australia, Mexico, Brazil, and Japan. Locate your local office at: **international.cengage.com/region**

Cengage Learning products are represented in Canada by Nelson Education, Ltd.

For your lifelong learning solutions, visit **www.cengage.com/custom**

Visit our corporate website at **www.cengage.com**

Printed in the United States of America

Table of Contents

Acknowledgments iv
Preface iv
Your Role in Learning 1
Your Group 1
Your Laboratory Instructor 2
Proposals and Class Discussions 3
Laboratory Notebooks 3
Scientific Reports 4

The Investigations

1. What Are the Safety Concerns in the Laboratory? 6
2. What's in the Flask? 19
3. How Is Lab Equipment Used? 23
4. Is the Water Hard or Soft? 27
5. How Can UV Sensitive Beads Be Used to Test Sunscreens? 31
6. How Much Cobalt Is in the Soil? 35
7. What Is a Copper Cycle? 39
8. What's in the Bottles? 43
9. How Hot Is the Water? 47
10. How Much Sodium Bicarbonate Is in the Mixture? 51
11. What Is the pH of Soil? 55
12. How Can a Battery Be Made from Coins? 59
13. Who Wrote the Ransom Note? 63
14. What Factors Affect Chemical Equilibrium? 67
15. What Formulation Makes the Best Toy? 71
16. How Can We Identify the Unknown Plastics? 75
    Presentations and Poster Sessions 79

Appendices

A. Automated Data Collection 83
B. Transmittance and Absorbance Data Collection 85
C. Measuring pH 88
D. Temperature Data Collection 91
E. Pressure Data Collection 92
F. Voltage Data Collection 94
G. Selected Laboratory Techniques 95
H. Laboratory Equipment 107
I. Sample Material Safety Data Sheet 108
J. Tables 114

Acknowledgments

The development of this manual involved the hard work of many people at Arizona State University and Scottsdale Community College. We would not have completed this book were it not for the contributions made by the students who piloted these experiments. We also want to thank the lab instructors for piloting these unconventional lab exercises, sometimes with little guidance about what to expect from students left on their own to design experiments. We especially wish to thank Jason Houtchens for his developmental work and writing *Investigation 16* (*How Can We Identify the Unknown Plastic?*). Many graduate students through the years have offered suggestions for improvements. We truly appreciate their insightful comments. Support staff at both institutions, in addition to their regular duties, helped in the preparation of student and instructor materials during the piloting stage of development. Finally, we would like to thank the editorial staff at Brooks/Cole for its help in developing this work.

Preface

Chemistry is a discipline in which scientists inquire about the microscopic and macroscopic worlds around us to understand the chemical nature of our surroundings. The basis for this inquiry is experimentation in which chemists probe for answers to scientific questions we face in our world. Sometimes, chemists explore the microscopic world with well–established experimental techniques. More often, however, they must design their own experiments, adapting techniques to their specific problems. We hope that this laboratory experience helps you to develop important problem solving skills necessary for success in our competitive, technological society. With guidance from your laboratory instructor, the techniques described in this book, and your text book, you are free to use your creativity in solving the problems we pose here.

The inquiry-based investigations in this book are designed to foster your experimental problem solving skills as well as to help you learn laboratory techniques. Because of the experimental context, some things you do in the laboratory may not coincide directly with your lecture discussions. Some of the ideas you will confront in lab will not be examined in lecture because they are issues appropriate only for the laboratory. For example, we hope that this lab experience helps you develop experimental design skills. These skills are not easily developed in a lecture setting. While experimental skills depend on conceptual knowledge, they differ from the concepts you will learn in lecture. Some of the investigations will ask you to draw on conceptual information that may seem unfamiliar. Don't panic when you are confronted with these concepts. The textbook for the lecture component of this class will be a valuable resource in helping you relate the unfamiliar material to the problem at hand. Practicing scientists must often consult textual resources and colleagues to solve their problems. They often encounter difficulties, solutions for which are not neatly outlined in detailed laboratory procedures. Instead, they design their own experiments with the knowledge of experimental techniques in mind. Hopefully, this lab experience will expose you to the critical thinking skills used by practicing chemists; that is, we hope that from the lab experience you can "learn to learn," a skill demanded by employers of college graduates in any discipline.

Scientists and, indeed, members of nearly all other disciplines work in a community with others having similar interests. Employers are demanding that undergraduate education prepare future employees for working in a cooperative, team environment. In a spirit of collegiality, we have designed the laboratory investigations to maximize the contributions others can make in improving your understanding of chemistry and to prepare you for a workforce that depends on cooperative skills. These skills include communicating ideas, negotiating with others, valuing the contribution of all group members, and delegating tasks. During your laboratory meetings, you will draw from the understanding of your fellow students to help your group design and carry out the investigations. The group is responsible for the success of each individual in it.

In the laboratory you will be asked to draw on your knowledge of chemical concepts as well as your interpretation of appropriate experimental procedures. Because science is often a creative endeavor, we have removed the "recipes" that often accompany laboratory experiments in general chemistry. Planning investigations is often neglected in typical recipe experiments, where the design aspects are done by the experts who wrote the lab manual. These experts learned their experimental skills by trial, error, creativity, serendipity, and knowledge of chemical behavior. By removing the recipes we hope to encourage you to develop these critical skills. You are responsible, together with your fellow group members, for the overall planning of the experiment which includes the design, data collection, organization, interpretation, and communication of your laboratory investigations. This accountability will at times be frustrating because you may not feel intellectually equipped to complete the investigation. However, once you draw on your understanding of the world, the chemistry you have learned so far, and the experience of others, we are confident that you will find the investigations rewarding.

Richard C. Bauer
School of Letters and Sciences
Arizona State University
411 N. Central Ave. Suite 300
Phoenix, AZ 85004-0696
rbauer@asu.edu

James P. Birk
Department of Chemistry and Biochemistry
Arizona State University
PO Box 871604
Tempe, AZ 85287-1604
jbirk@asu.edu

Douglas J. Sawyer
Department of Chemistry
Scottsdale Community College
9000 E. Chaparral Rd.
Scottsdale, AZ 85256
doug.sawyer@sccmail.maricopa.edu

Your Role in Learning

We have found that successful chemistry students do some chemistry every day. Does a college basketball team practice once a week for ten hours? No, the team practices several times a week for shorter durations. You should approach your study of chemistry in the same manner; that is, practice chemistry every day for a little while instead of doing marathon cramming sessions once a week. The laboratory provides you with an opportunity to practice your chemical understanding in class while you plan and conduct your investigations with your team members. Indeed, your laboratory success depends on your understanding of chemical concepts, your ability to regularly put your understanding into practice, and your capacity to communicate your ideas orally and in writing. Don't be afraid to voice your ideas during your lab meetings and when your group meets outside of class. Putting your thoughts into words is a critical exercise in helping you develop cognitive skills. Also, your fellow students and your instructor can help you make better sense of the material provided they know what you understand about the subject at hand.

As stated previously, we hope the lab environment helps you to draw on the experience of others in the course. Hopefully, your fellow group members will help you succeed in this course. Likewise, you are responsible for the success of each team member. You must take your role in your team seriously for you and your fellow group members to succeed. Just as individuals are accountable for their work in the "real" world, so too will you be held personally responsible for gaining an understanding of laboratory procedure and chemistry concepts.

As in other disciplines, learning chemistry requires your active immersion in the discipline. No matter how good (or bad) your instructor or lab partners are, your personal commitment to the course is the key to your success in chemistry.

Your Group

The organizational structure of most companies is team based. Employers have found that in a team-structured environment, gains are made by people putting their heads together to solve problems. In educational settings, group-based, cooperative learning efforts improve relations across different cultures and genders, increase student retention in difficult science courses, and generally improve students' performance. In industrial, governmental, and educational institutions, group work often has at least four characteristics: (1) the group works toward a common goal, (2) the group is responsible for the success of each member, (3) each member is individually accountable for completing various tasks and gaining relevant knowledge, and (4) the group members share resources. At the beginning of the course your instructor will assign you to a group in which you will conduct the investigations throughout the semester. You will act as a team of investigators to solve the assigned problems posed in this book. Socially, you may not have anything in common with other members of your group. However, successful team efforts often rest on the ability to draw from the experiences of people from diverse backgrounds.

To facilitate your group's success, each member could assume one of the following roles:

Team leader — coordinates the activities of group members, including the generation of reports.

Assistant leader — keeps the group on task. Consolidates supporting literature relevant to the investigation. Monitors group activities so all members contribute in a healthy, supportive environment.

Data collection expert — directs the data collection activities for the group. This includes identifying the information that must be collected and recording the data in an appropriately organized manner.

Experimental technique expert — determines the appropriate reagents and equipment assembly for data collection. Consults with instructor for special instructions about equipment.

After each investigation these duties should rotate so each group member has an opportunity to develop the associated skills of each role. Even though you will assume various roles, each group member is expected to contribute to experimental design discussions. Your instructor will monitor your group's activities so all members take part.

Because each member of your group is individually accountable for successful completion of the class assignments, you will be asked to describe your contribution to each investigation. At the end of each investigation is a contribution form that must be completed by every member of the group. On that form you will report your percent effort as well as your perception of what other group members contributed. In addition, you will also describe what you did to help your group complete the investigation and write the report. The contribution forms are due at the same time as your report.

Your Laboratory Instructor

In light of our goal to promote creative student development of experimental design and technique, your laboratory instructor will serve as a resource, not as a dictator of "correct" problem solutions. Do not expect your instructor to tell you exactly what to do. Your success in the course depends on your ability to think for yourself. Too much input from your instructor will undermine the learning process during your laboratory investigations. Use all the resources at your disposal before you approach your instructor with questions. These resources include the lab book, your textbook, your fellow students, the Internet, and your library. However, when you are uncertain of specific techniques or unfamiliar with laboratory equipment, consult your instructor before carrying out your experiment. Once your experimental design is in order, you **must** get your instructor's approval before proceeding with your investigation.

Proposals and Class Discussions

Many of the investigations in this manual are designed to be completed in two weeks. The first week of an investigation will involve designing your experiment to solve the problems posed. This is not a trivial task, so you can expect it to take some time. You must consider equipment issues, determine which reagents and quantities you will use, and decide on variables to control, data to collect, and how you will analyze the data. In addition, you must also address safety considerations. Once your group has decided on an experimental design, you will need to present your ideas to your instructor. Your instructor may require a written proposal before your actual experimentation begins. Your proposal should address how the experiment will yield a solution to the problem. You should describe the data you will collect and materials and quantities you will use. Finally, you must describe the safety hazards associated with your experiment and appropriate precautions you will take to avoid personal injury. There may be times when you want to begin by running simple experiments to make observations or by collecting preliminary data before you decide on your experimental design. It is perfectly acceptable to run a simple initial experiment but you must obtain the instructor's approval before you proceed.

At various points during the investigation your instructor may ask each group of students to give a short progress report orally to the rest of the class, much as practicing chemists do in scientific meetings. These reports may occur midway through an investigation or at the end. Part of your grade will be based on the clarity and creativity of your presentation.

Laboratory Notebooks

Scientists maintain laboratory notebooks as a permanent record of their laboratory activities. They always refer back to them when, for example, they apply for patents or compose scientific papers. Additionally, lab notebooks are often used in litigation when scientific laboratories are taken to court. Because of these important implications it is imperative to learn data collection and recording techniques that prepare you for future scientific study. Careful recording of experimental observations and results will be encouraged and enforced. You should develop a style of notebook that is both convenient for yourself and intelligible to others. There are some features of the format that are dictated by universal convention, while others are largely a matter of personal taste. There is an inevitable tendency to make temporary records or to trust your memory, presumably to make the final copy look neater, but this is a bad habit which you should avoid. Those aspects of the format for recording data that must be observed are all related to the idea that the notebook should be a permanent, documented, and primary record of laboratory observations. Use the following guidelines in maintaining your lab notebooks:

1. Research data are kept in bound notebooks with prenumbered pages. Because of limited space at your lab station, your instructor may permit you to have a spiral bound lab notebook. The notebook should be dedicated to a single subject. Your instructor may want your notebook to contain carbonless duplicates that can be torn out and turned in.

2. The lab notebook will serve as a permanent record of what you did, data you collected, and observations you made in the laboratory. Someone wanting to duplicate your experiment

should be able to do so using your notebook. You should also include calculations and summaries.

3. All entries should be written permanently in ink. Mark out mistakes with a single line.

4. Sign and date each page.

5. Leave the first page blank to include a table of contents.

6. In lieu of rewriting a lab procedure, it is acceptable to cut and paste a copy of the procedure into the lab notebook with appropriate references.

7. Some of the data you collect may be processed with a computer. You may paste the printout of the data in your lab notebook. However, in your lab notebooks you must still make a written record of the data you collect and observations you make. Your instructor will occasionally inspect your data and observations from your lab notebooks.

8. While your group will have a data collection expert for each investigation, each student must maintain a record of data collected. The manner in which you obtain data from your group is at your discretion.

Scientific Reports

The scientific report is one manner in which investigators communicate results of their experiments. They are usually written in impersonal or third person, passive voice. You will be required to write laboratory reports about your work to give you practice in transmitting scientific results to others. A report should be brief and to the point, and should be readable, both grammatically and stylistically. Reports must be typed. Your report will be judged on the quality of your work as well as on its presentation, its interpretation, and the reasoning behind the interpretation. While the exact format of the report is up to you, the report should contain the items listed below (assuming they are appropriate to the experiment). The format given below is that generally used for the reporting of scientific results.

Introduction: This should contain a clear statement of the problem, its goals, and your general approach to solving the problem. A typical introduction might be a short paragraph in length. As you do more original work, the significance of the present work in the context of what is known should be stated. Most scientific papers include a discussion of background theory in the introduction. Your instructor may direct you to include this information. Do not copy the goals listed for the investigations in your report introduction. Those goals merely represent a checklist of items to complete during the investigation. The opening question in the investigation title should provide a guide fro writing you introduction.

Experimental: Enough detail should be given in this section so that someone else, not otherwise familiar with the work, could repeat the experiments. Do not write your experimental section in second person voice. You are describing what you did, not providing directions for someone else to follow.

(a)   You must identify all materials used. Include any information you have on the purity and concentrations of the materials. You should list reagents, such as acids, bases, and solvents, that are normally available, but you need not describe them in detail. You should give formulas of all compounds, together with their chemical names, at least once.

(b)   Unless it is standard equipment, you should describe apparatus, with a drawing if necessary, and with names and sources of specific equipment if they are not widely known. You should list commercially available equipment, but you need not describe it in detail.

(c)   Include a description of how the work was done. For experiments involving established procedures, reference to the appropriate source of the procedure may suffice. You should include all the background data, equations, and formulas necessary to the experiment.

Results: For most reports, the presentation of the results and the discussion of their significance may be separated into two distinct sections. Occasionally, however, a chronological approach might be preferable. Regardless of the outline you follow, several points should be noted:

(a) The major experimental results, including the original data, the calculated results, and at least one detailed sample calculation showing how the final results were obtained should be presented. It may be appropriate to include the theory behind your calculations. Include only relevant data and describe assumptions you made in the collection of the data. Introduce equations, figures, graphs, and tables where necessary for clarity and conciseness.

(b) All numerical data should be reported in accepted, self-consistent systems of units. Report the precision of the work, theoretical values if known, and the relative error of the experimental result.

Discussion (or Conclusions): You should discuss your results in detail.

(a) In the discussion of the significance of the results, an objective explanation is essential. You should point out the limitations of the work. You should also interpret, compare, and contrast your results with reports available from other sources. Background theory should be used to explain your results. Try to correlate your results with the chemical principles or reactions involved.

(b) If your results differ significantly from expected values, or if the precision is worse than should be obtained with your procedure, discuss the possible sources of error in detail.

(c) A summary adds to the value of the presentation. It should be interpretive and not repetitious. Discuss how the results relate to the goals of the experiment and any conclusions that may be drawn from the experiment. Consider any alternate conclusions or explanations. The problem may not have been solved completely; if so, you might suggest an approach or a refinement that could be used for further study.

Investigation 1
What Are the Safety Concerns in the Laboratory?

Introduction

Working in a chemistry laboratory has certain inherent dangers. You can avoid laboratory hazards with the proper knowledge of the materials and chemicals with which you will be working. In this investigation you will acquaint yourself with safety rules implemented for the protection of everyone in the lab. In the event that a dangerous situation does arise, this investigation provides guidelines for dealing with these occurrences. In addition to answering the questions on the worksheet, you will identify the safety rules that your team believes are the most important.

Goals

As you complete this investigation you will:
1. Become familiar with rules designed to maintain a safe laboratory environment.
2. Become familiar with procedures for handling chemicals.
3. Select the safety rules that you think are most important and must be followed at all times.
4. Informally summarize your chosen safety rules in class discussion and formally write up your conclusions in a report.

Materials

Reading materials in this investigation
Other materials provided by your instructor

Getting Started

Based on the materials provided, and a tour of the lab, work with your group to develop answers to all of the questions on the worksheet at the end of this investigation. If you are uncertain of an answer, check it with your instructor. Work with your group to select the five rules that you think are most important to ensure your safety during laboratory sessions. Be prepared to discuss at least one of your chosen safety rules with the rest of your class.

Report

As a group, review the safety rules and answer the questions on the worksheet. Each student must submit answers to the worksheet questions at the end of the lab period. In addition, your group must submit a report justifying your team's five most important safety rules. Your written report should include a one-paragraph justification for each of your choices and how you will attend to these rules every time you work in the lab. The report must be typed and grammatically correct. It will be returned to you for corrections if it is not acceptable. Each member of the group should be prepared to discuss your selections with the rest of the class.

Safety Rules and Laboratory Procedures

For many of the investigations you will complete in this lab class, your instructor will relate specific safety information regarding the chemicals or procedures you will use. Instructors will do their best to provide a safe working environment for all the students. However, you have a responsibility to everyone in the lab to understand and follow the safety rules listed below. For everyone's protection, your instructor will strictly enforce the safety rules. Failure to abide by them may result in your dismissal from the class.

- *Plan your investigations in advance.* Many lab accidents occur because the experiment is poorly planned or disorganized. A well-planned experiment not only reduces accidental risk, but will also ensure that your data collection will proceed in a smooth manner.

- *Experiments must be approved by your instructor.* While we encourage creativity in solving the problems we pose in this manual, your instructor *must* approve your experimental designs. Each investigation requires a formal proposal to your instructor before you can proceed with your experiments. (See page 2 for a discussion of lab proposals.) Your instructor will approve your proposal after careful consideration and discussion of safety implications. If you choose to modify a common procedure, your modification must also be approved by your instructor.

- *Never work in the laboratory alone or without your instructor present.* If an accident occurs an authority must be present to hasten medical attention. Also, you should always be present while your experiments are in progress.

- *Food and beverages are not allowed in the laboratory.* Even if you plan to consume them outside of lab, you run the risk of chemical contamination. This applies to chewing gum and chewing tobacco, as well. You should store your personal effects away from your work area.

- *Smoking in the laboratory is prohibited*, for obvious reasons. Flammable solvents are often present in the lab and can easily explode or ignite in the presence of a flame. You also run the risk of chemical contamination of your cigarettes (as if they don't already have enough toxic chemicals in them).

- *Immediately report all injuries, including minor ones, to your instructor.* The presence of chemicals can complicate even minor cuts.

- *Recommendation: Get health insurance.* We recommend that anyone enrolled in a chemistry course obtain personal health insurance. Enrollment in courses does not automatically entitle you to insurance coverage if an accident occurs in the lab. If your campus has a health center it may be capable of treating some injuries. However, further medical attention may require your transport to other facilities. You may be responsible for the cost of those additional services.

Safety Equipment and Laboratory Attire

The prevention of accidents for you personal safety should be your first priority when you conduct laboratory experiments. Your instructor will strictly enforce safety rules regarding appropriate safety equipment and attire.

- *You must wear safety goggles at all times while experimental work is in progress in the laboratory*, even if you have completed your experimentation. Many injuries occur because of flying debris or splashed chemicals originating some distance from the victim. Safety glasses are unacceptable for eye protection in a chemistry laboratory. In addition, you should not wear contact lenses in a chemical laboratory. Chemicals can splash under the lens and cause permanent damage to the cornea. Furthermore, noxious gases can permeate soft lenses.

- *Make every effort to protect your bare skin.* Minimally, you should wear long pants, shirts with sleeves, and shoes. We also advise you to wear a plastic apron or a lab coat to protect you and your clothing from corrosive chemicals. Restrain loose clothing, hair, and jewelry to prevent injury. For protection against broken glass or spilled chemicals, *wear shoes at all times in the laboratory.* Sandals or open-toed shoes are not appropriate footwear for the laboratory.

- *Identify the location of the safety equipment such as safety showers, eyewashes, fire extinguishers, first-aid kits, respiratory equipment, and emergency exits.* Your instructor will call your attention to these items during your first laboratory period. You should understand how safety equipment is used.

Cleanliness

- *Keep your assigned bench area neat and free of spilled chemicals.* A messy bench is a potential safety hazard. An unorganized bench also leads to confusion that prohibits the efficient running of the investigation. Experiments will proceed more rapidly and safely in a neatly kept area. When you enter the laboratory it should be clean. If not, you must clean your area before you proceed. You must also leave the lab clean when you depart.

- *Spilled chemicals must be cleaned up immediately.* Occasional spillage is unavoidable and will cause no damage if it is immediately sponged off with water. However, many solutions and solids will attack the bench sides and tops if allowed to remain on them for any length of time. Spills can also cause chemical burns if you accidentally rub against them. If you spill a large volume of water or other liquid it must also be cleaned up immediately. If the material is corrosive or flammable, ask the instructor for assistance. If acids or bases are spilled on the floor or bench, neutralize with solid sodium bicarbonate, then dilute with water. Mercury is very toxic, even in small quantities (for example, from broken thermometers). Notify the instructor immediately in case of any spillage of mercury.

- *You must dispose of all laboratory waste in appropriate containers.* EPA regulations require that all chemical waste be disposed of properly. Failure to comply with EPA standards has resulted in heavy fines leveled on individuals as well as institutions. In planning your experiments, keep in the mind the waste implications of your selected design. Waste bottles for each experiment will be provided by your instructor. They will be labeled according to the specific contents that should be placed inside. *Flammable liquids should be disposed of in specially marked bottles*, never in the sink. Do not place any materials in the sink since damaging overflows may result. Keep lab sinks and troughs clean at all times. *Broken glass should be discarded in the special containers provided.* Ask your instructor for assistance if necessary.

- *Clean your bench area and common lab areas before you leave.* Make certain that the gas and water sources are turned off and that your drawer (if you have one) is closed and locked. Always use clean apparatus for each experiment. Dirty equipment is harder to clean later and will require considerable scrubbing the next time it is needed. Clean glassware by scrubbing with a brush, hot water, and detergent, then make a final rinse with a stream of distilled water. Do not dry glassware with compressed air because it is often oily.

- *Return any special equipment* which you obtained for an experiment (for example, hardware, rubber stoppers, rubber tubing, test tubes, files, volumetric flasks, and so on) at the end of the laboratory period to the location from which it was obtained. Students in other periods will probably need to use this equipment.

Laboratory Procedures

- *Balances*: Keep the balances and the surrounding area clean. *Never place chemicals directly on the balance pans*. Instead, place a piece of paper or a small container on the pan first, then weigh your material. Never weigh an object while it is hot because of the danger to you and to equipment. Also, the hot item creates air currents around the balance that can lead to inaccurate mass measurements.

- *Pipetting: Never pipet any liquid directly by mouth!* Use a rubber bulb instead. The convenience of mouth pipetting is not worth the risk of ingesting toxic chemicals.

- *Burners: Avoid burns by lighting burners properly.* After checking that the gas jet was not left open from a previous class, turn on the gas. Light the match away from the burner. Slowly move the lit match to just over the side of the barrel top, keeping your hand and fingers away from the flame area. Be careful when near the flame — especially watch loose clothing.

hottest part of flame

air adjustment

gas inlet

- *Heating: Always use a test tube holder when heating a substance in a test tube as shown in the picture. Be careful not to direct the tube toward yourself or anyone nearby.* A suddenly formed bubble of vapor may eject the contents violently and dangerously. *Never apply the direct heat of a flame to heavy glassware* such as volumetric flasks, burets, graduated cylinders, bottles, mortars, pestles, and thermometers. These items can break spectacularly when heated strongly. Volumetric glassware also becomes distorted from the calibrated volumes. Avoid heating any object too suddenly. Apply the flame intermittently at first.

Give heated objects adequate cooling time. During any procedure involving the heating of an object, avoid burns by thinking twice before touching anything. *Give heated glass adequate time to cool*; it looks cool long before it is safe to handle. Use the appropriate type of tongs when moving hot objects. Test tube holders should be used for test tubes only, as they are too weak to carry flasks or other heavier objects.

- *Glass tubing:* The most common laboratory accidents occur because of improper insertion of glass objects into rubber stoppers. If you intend to insert a piece of glass tubing or a thermometer into a hole in a rubber stopper, *lubricate the glass tubing* with a drop of glycerin or water, *hold the tubing in your hand close to the hole, and keep the entire assembly wrapped in a towel while applying gentle pressure with a twisting motion. Use only tubing which has been fire polished.*

Chemicals

- *Always consult proper documentation before working with any chemical.* OSHA regulations require that Material Safety Data Sheets (MSDSs) be available to those working with chemicals. Your instructor will show you where the MSDSs are located. A sample can be found in Appendix I of this manual. There are good Web sites that have MSDSs (for example, see *http://www.fisher1.com*). At the beginning of each investigation your instructor will discuss the dangerous properties of any materials for which special precautions are necessary.

- *All chemicals should be considered as potentially toxic. Never taste a chemical or solution.* If you are asked to smell a chemical, *gently fan the vapors toward your nose.* You might ask your instructor to demonstrate the proper procedure for smelling a chemical. Nearly all chemicals are poisonous to the human body to some extent. Latex gloves are available to protect your hands from chemicals that may irritate the skin.

- *All chemicals which come in contact with the skin should be considered toxic and immediately washed off* with soap and copious quantities of water. If the area of contact is large, use the safety shower. If the eyes are splashed with a liquid, immediately flush with the eyewash. Many toxic organic compounds, which are not corrosive, are absorbed through the skin with no immediately visible symptoms. Make a habit of washing your hands before leaving the laboratory and never remove any chemicals from the laboratory. If you receive a chemical burn, after washing with water, seek medical treatment.

- *When diluting concentrated acids, always pour the acid slowly into the water with continuous stirring.* Heat is liberated in the dilution process and if water is poured into acid, steam may form with explosive violence, causing splattering.

- *Use the fume hood for all experiments involving poisonous or objectionable gases or vapors.* Never purposely allow fumes or volatile liquids to escape into the open room. Inhalation of more than a slight dose of such fumes should be reported and you should get to fresh air immediately. Also get fresh air if you are exposed to lab fumes for prolonged time periods.

- *Never use an open flame and flammable liquids at the same time.* Also, if your procedure calls for use of a flammable liquid, carry out the experiment in the hood. Do not heat anything other than water or an aqueous solution directly over an open flame. Consider all solvents other than water at least as flammable as gasoline. Many, such as ether, are more flammable.

7. Describe the location of the nearest

   (a) safety shower.

   (b) eyewash fountain.

   (c) fire extinguisher.

   (d) first-aid kit.

   (e) emergency exit.

8. What should you do if chemicals are spilled on lab benches?

9. What should you do if you spill some mercury?

10. What are the consequences of drying glassware with compressed air?

11. What are proper procedures for weighing chemicals on balances?

12. Why should you always use a rubber bulb when pipetting?

13. How should you dispose of

    (a) acids and bases?

    (b) aqueous solutions?

    (c) small amounts of water-soluble solids?

    (d) large amounts of water-soluble solids?

    (e) insoluble solids?

    (f) broken glass?

    (g) flammable liquids?

14. Describe the procedure for inserting glass tubing into a rubber stopper.

15. Why should you never heat heavy-walled glassware (volumetric flasks, burets, graduated cylinders, and so on) directly with a flame?

16. How should you move a hot flask? Why is a test tube holder inappropriate?

17. How should you smell a chemical?

18. What should be your immediate reaction if chemicals come into contact with your skin?

19. When is it appropriate to taste a chemical or solution?

20. Should you pour acid into water or water into acid? Why?

21. When should you use the fume hood?

22. What precautions must be taken when working with flammable liquids?

23. What are the consequences of returning unused chemicals to the reagent bottles?

24. What information is generally provided on a MSDS? With a chemical of your choice, look up the proper handling procedure for that chemical.

What Are the Safety Concerns in the Laboratory? **Team Contribution Form**

Identify the percent contribution each team member made in this investigation, listing your name first.

Name: Percent Contribution:

_____   _____

_____   _____

_____   _____

_____   _____

Describe your contribution to the completion of the investigation and the writing of the report.

Return this sheet to your lab instructor.

Investigation 2
What's in the Flask?

Introduction

Chemists often spend time designing experiments to determine the identity of unknown substances. For example, environmental chemists analyze water samples obtained from water treatment facilities. They design their experiments to determine the identity of the substances present in the liquid and the relative abundance of each component. In this experiment you will hone your investigative skills while you become acquainted with the planning stages of experimental work.

Part 1

Suppose your team of chemists has been contacted by a municipal water supplier to recommend procedures for determining the identity of an unknown liquid. A sample has been obtained and placed in the laboratory. Your task is to design experimental procedures that could characterize the unknown's purity, physical properties, and chemical behavior. All of these may ultimately help in revealing the identity of the liquid.

Part 2

In addition to designing experiments to identify the unknown, you will become acquainted with making laboratory measurements by determining the densities of cold tap water, hot water, ice, and an unknown solid.

Goals

As you complete this investigation you will:
1. Design experiments that will identify the composition of an unknown liquid.
2. Determine the densities of cold tap water, hot tap water, and ice.
3. Determine the density of an unknown solid.
4. Write a report that provides reasonable explanations for observed differences in densities.

Materials

Unknown liquid
Unknown solid
Graduated cylinders
Beakers
Lab balances
Rulers
Other miscellaneous lab equipment

Getting Started

Part 1

In planning your investigation to identify the composition of the unknown liquid, you can assume that standard experimental equipment is at your disposal. You will also be able to consult with your fellow investigators. Your team will submit a proposal to your instructor that includes ways you would determine the properties of the liquid and justification for your procedures. Also, include advantages and disadvantages for your selected experiments. Your proposal must be legibly written in standard English following accepted grammatical and spelling rules. You will not actually carry out your experiments unless permission has been granted by your instructor.

Part 2

Design an experiment to determine the density of the tap water in your lab. Since density is defined as mass per unit volume you will have to measure both those quantities. You may want to consult your textbook for further information about density. Determine the density of ice and compare it to the density of liquid water. Also, determine the density of the unknown solid.

Before carrying out your density determinations, submit a brief proposal to your instructor for approval. Use the guidelines described on page 2 for generating a proposal.

Report

For *Part 1* of this investigation, turn in your group's ideas for identification of the unknown liquid in the form of a proposal as directed by your instructor. For *Part 2*, you will write a formal report about the density experiments your group ran. Your report should clearly state what you found regarding the densities of water, ice, and the unknown solid. In addition to writing your report according to the criteria described on pages 4 and 5 of this lab manual, your discussion should address the items listed below. Try to explain differences in observed densities by considering microscopic arrangements of the atoms or molecules involved in the materials you studied. In your final report you should address the following items:

- Does the density of water from the hot water tap differ from that of the cold water? If it does, explain why.
- Explain the difference between the density of the solid and the density of water.

Caution:
While working in the laboratory wear your goggles at all times.
You do not know the identity of the unknown liquid so use
caution if you decide to handle the bottle.

What's in the Flask? **Team Contribution Form**

Identify the percent contribution each team member made in this investigation, listing your name first.

Name: Percent Contribution:

_____   _____

_____   _____

_____   _____

_____   _____

Describe your contribution to the completion of the investigation and the writing of the report.

Return this sheet to your lab instructor.

Investigation 3
How Is Lab Equipment Used?

Introduction

When planning a given experiment, equipment and techniques used to collect data should offer approximately the same precision. The overall precision of an experiment is determined by the least precise of the measurements you make. Therefore, if you use a piece of equipment that is known to be imprecise, you should not waste time by making other measurements more precisely.

Suppose the supplier of the equipment in your instructional laboratory has recently contracted for your team's services to test the volumetric precision and accuracy of items they have supplied. The equipment includes burets, pipets, volumetric flasks, graduated cylinders, graduated beakers, medicine droppers, and other equipment as directed by your instructor. The manufacturing equipment for each of these lab items is of unknown quality so the measurement ability of these devices is suspect. Assuming that the balance in your lab has been recently calibrated, it is the only piece of equipment you can trust.

Goals

As you complete this investigation you will:
1. Determine proper procedures to weigh equipment and chemicals.
2. Determine proper procedures to measure out specific volumes of liquids.
3. Determine the measurement precision and accuracy of the items sent by the customer.
4. Compare the number of significant figures in values measured with different techniques.
5. Report your results as directed by your instructor.

Materials

Water	Droppers
Electronic balance	Sand
Weighing bottles, papers, and/or boats	1-L beaker
Beakers, volumetric flasks, graduated cylinders,	Other supplies by request
pipets, burets, and other volumetric glassware	

Getting Started

In this investigation your group has to develop a procedure to determine the precision and accuracy of various volume measuring equipment. Because the only item in the lab that you can trust is a balance, your procedure will have to involve a relationship between mass and volume. (Hint: Density is a relationship between mass and volume. You might look up density in your textbook. The density of water as it varies with temperature can be found in Appendix J.) As you develop your procedure, keep in mind that you must test both the precision and accuracy of the volume measuring equipment as directed by your instructor. How many trials should you run for each item? To become adept at using the available balances you should develop a procedure for weighing out exactly 1 gram of sand. If you have more than one type of balance in your lab, learn how to use all that are available. (Treat the sand as though it were a corrosive chemical, such as sodium hydroxide.) *Chemicals should never be weighed directly on a balance pan!*

Once you have studied the accuracy and precision of the volume measuring items, develop procedures for measuring exact quantities of liquids. Specifically, how would determine the volume and mass of 1 drop of water? How would you measure exactly 10 mL of water using different lab equipment. How would you measure exactly 100 mL of water? Try different procedures to determine what works best. (Treat the water as though it were a corrosive chemical, such as sulfuric acid.)

Other Activities

To further explore uses of lab equipment, complete the tasks below as directed by your instructor. Comment on these items in an appendix to your lab report.

1. Develop a procedure for weighing exactly 1 liter of water in a large beaker. What factors cause difficulties in carrying out this procedure with the equipment available in the lab?
2. Suppose a hospital supply company that prepares solutions for use in intravenous (IV) bags has asked for your help in the preparation of saline (sodium chloride) solutions. A typical IV bag contains 0.900 mass percent sodium chloride. The company usually begins from a solution that is 9.00 mass percent sodium chloride. It wants your help in developing a procedure for preparing 10.0 kilograms of 0.900% solution from the 9.00% starting solution. How would you tell them to prepare the saline solution? Your procedure should include recommendations about the proper measuring equipment.

Report

The report must be typed and grammatically correct. Within the appropriate sections of your report, be sure to address all the questions asked in this investigation. Your report may be returned to you for corrections if it is not acceptable. Reports should be constructed according to the format described on pages 4 and 5 in this manual (unless directed otherwise by your instructor), to the extent that this format is appropriate to the experiments that you designed. The emphasis of this report is on your recommendations regarding laboratory procedures so the *Experimental* section should be clear. When writing the report keep in mind the goals of the investigation — in this case, recommendations to a supply company regarding use of its equipment. You should include an explanation about the circumstances under which each item should be used. Finally, you should compare your results to those obtained by other students.

> **Caution:**
> **While working in the laboratory wear your goggles at all times.**

How Is Lab Equipment Used? **Team Contribution Form**

Identify the percent contribution each team member made in this investigation, listing your name first.

Name: Percent Contribution:

_____   _____

_____   _____

_____   _____

_____   _____

Describe your contribution to the completion of the investigation and the writing of the report.

Return this sheet to your instructor.

Investigation 4
Is the Water Hard or Soft?

Introduction

Homeowners frequently hear from telemarketers peddling everything from magazines to vacuum cleaners. Telemarketers for water purification systems seem especially common lately. They offer free testing of household water in hopes that they can show that an expensive water softener should be purchased. A consumer advocate wishing to help homeowners test their own water has asked for your group's help in developing a technique for testing water hardness at home.

To determine if a home really needs an expensive new water softener, you should address several questions. How do you know whether your water is hard or soft? How hard is it? Which chemicals work to soften the water? As a group, your team will investigate the above concerns. The technique you develop might be endorsed by a consumer advocate company.

Goals

As you complete this investigation you will:
1. Develop a method for determining the hardness of a water sample.
2. Use this method to measure the temporary and permanent hardness of the water.
3. Use this method to measure the relative effectiveness of various chemicals as water softeners.
4. Report your results as directed by your instructor

Materials

$0.00100\ M\ CaCl_2$ solution, which has a hardness of 100 ppm
Soap solution
Water sample
Distilled water sample
Borax, $Na_2B_4O_7(s)$
Sodium chloride, $NaCl(s)$
Sodium carbonate (washing soda), $Na_2CO_3(s)$
Sodium phosphate, $Na_3PO_4(s)$
Sodium sulfate, $Na_2SO_4(s)$
Plastic droppers
Balances
Graduated cylinders, burets, pipets, or other volume measuring devices
Other supplies by request

Getting Started

Water that contains the impurities Ca^{2+}, Mg^{2+}, and sometimes Fe^{3+}, along with the anions Cl^-, SO_4^{2-}, and HCO_3^-, is called *hard water* because the metal ions cause an undesirable precipitate of soap scum when soap is added. For example, some soaps contain compounds of the anion, $C_{17}H_{35}CO_2^-$. This anion can react with calcium ions present in hard water to make an insoluble compound:

$$2C_{17}H_{35}CO_2^-(aq) + Ca^{2+}(aq) \rightarrow Ca(C_{17}H_{35}CO_2)_2(s)$$

Lathering will not occur until the metal ions associated with water hardness are consumed. The formation of a permanent lather can be used as a measure of the hardness of the water. When developing your method for determining hardness, however, be sure to consider whether suds would form with the first addition of soap in the absence of any hardness. You might begin by comparing the hardness of tap water and deionized or distilled water. A solution of 0.00100 *M* calcium chloride is provided. This solution has a hardness of 100 part per million. This solution can be used as a hard water standard to quantify your results.

Hardness is considered to be permanent if it remains after water is boiled. Hardness that is removed by boiling is called *temporary hardness*. The temporary hardness is caused by bicarbonate compounds, which are converted to insoluble carbonate compounds by heating:

$$Ca^{2+}(aq) + 2HCO_3^-(aq) + heat \rightarrow CaCO_3(s) + CO_2(g) + H_2O(l)$$

Since the calcium is removed as a carbonate precipitate, it is no longer present as free calcium ions in solution. Permanent hardness is caused by chloride or sulfate salts, which are not changed by heating.

When testing the use of various solid chemicals as water softeners, be sure to compare equal amounts of the solids and make sure that the solids are completely dissolved.

Report

Submit a report as directed by your instructor. It may be returned to you for corrections if it is not acceptable. Your discussion should address the different types of hardness and the relative efficiency of the various salts as water softeners. You should also compare various water-softening systems, such as the new magnetic systems and older methods such as ion exchange, distillation, and reverse osmosis. Useful information about water softening can be found on the internet. Compare the costs of the different systems. Could you use inexpensive chemicals to soften the water?

Caution:
While working in the laboratory wear your goggles at all times.

Is the Water Hard or Soft? **Team Contribution Report Form**

Identify the percent contribution each team member made in this investigation, listing your name first.

Name: Percent Contribution:

_____   _____

_____   _____

_____   _____

_____   _____

Describe your contribution to the completion of this investigation and the writing of the report.

Return this sheet to your lab instructor.

Introduction

Ultraviolet light from the harsh rays of the sun has led to development of a variety of skin and eye protection products. During the summer, drug store counters often display UV protection lotions that range from 2 to 35 on the SPF scale. In addition to the skin, eyes must be protected from the damaging UV rays of the sun.

A company that develops UV protective products has begun testing a new experimental protocol. They believe that UV sensitive beads can serve as a surface for testing their skin care products. Unfortunately, they have had little success in developing an experimental procedure that makes use of these beads. Because of your laboratory skills, the company has contracted the services of your group to develop a procedure to use UV sensitive beads for testing the efficacy of sunscreens. In addition, the company wants you to use the beads to test the UV protection of sunglasses.

Goals

As you complete this investigation you will:
1. Develop a method for using UV sensitive beads to test sunscreens.
2. Use your method to test and compare various sunscreens.
3. Test various sunglasses for UV protection. (You may have to bring these from home.)
4. Report your results as directed by your instructor.

Materials

UV sensitive beads of various colors
Sunscreens ranging in SPF protection
Soap
Cheese cloth or other fabrics
Plastic bags and/or plastic wrap
UV lamp
Balances
Other supplies by request

Getting Started

In this investigation you will develop a procedure for using UV sensitive beads to test sunscreens. You might begin by observing what happens to the beads when exposed to the sun or when placed near a UV lamp. How long does it take for the beads to change color? Is direct exposure to the sun necessary to change the color of the beads? Do you get better results working in the shade? After you get a feel for how the beads behave in the presence of UV light, determine how you might use them to test sunscreens for UV protection. As you design your procedure, consider what variables to control. What will you use as a control for a basis of comparison?

In addition to testing sunscreens, observe what happens when the UV light is filtered through various kinds of glass. For example, what happens when the beads are placed in a glass bottle or under eye glasses? What happens when UV light is filtered through sun glasses?

Report

Submit a report as directed by your instructor. It should include a discussion of your method for using UV sensitive beads to test sunscreens and sunglasses. Remember that the company wants your recommendations for an experimental protocol.

Caution:
While working in the laboratory wear your goggles at all times.
Protect your eyes from the UV lamp.

Can UV Sensitive Beads be Used to Test Sunscreens? **Team Contribution Report Form**

Identify the percent contribution each team member made in this investigation, listing your name first.

Name: Percent Contribution:

_____   _____

_____   _____

_____   _____

_____   _____

Describe your contribution to the completion of this investigation and the writing of the report.

Return this sheet to your lab instructor.

Investigation 6
How Much Cobalt Is in the Soil?

Introduction

A group of dairy farmers has recently reported to its county cooperative extension service that its animals appear sick. Based on the symptoms, the county suspects that the cows are suffering from a cobalt deficiency. Cobalt(II) is required for production of vitamin B_{12}. Proper animal diet requires the soil to contain 0.13 to 0.30 mg cobalt per kg of soil. Soils that do not meet this condition can be amended with careful addition of cobalt nitrate or other cobalt compounds. Because it lacks the proper equipment, the county extension service has contracted for your team to determine the amount of cobalt(II) in a solution sent to your lab. To get representative samples, the extension service collected 2.00 kg of soil from 20 different farms in the county. The cobalt was then extracted from the soil, dissolved in water, and concentrated by a factor of 10,000 to prepare 1 L of solution. Because the cobalt ion is a colored species in water, spectroscopic techniques can be used to determine the concentration of cobalt(II) in an unknown solution.

Goals

As you complete this investigation you will:
1. Prepare a standard plot of absorbance versus known cobalt(II) nitrate concentrations.
2. Determine the concentration of cobalt(II) in the solution obtained from a soil sample.
3. Determine if cobalt nitrate should be added to the soil. If so, how much will be required to meet the necessary nutritional needs of the animals?
4. Report your findings to the cooperative extension service as directed by your instructor.

Materials

0.1 M^* Co(NO$_3$)$_2$(aq)   Cuvettes
Unknown cobalt(II) solution   Tissues (preferably lint free)
Volume measuring equipment   Other supplies by request
Device to measure light absorbance
      *Obtain exact concentration from the reagent bottle.

Getting Started

For information about the basics of spectroscopy, see Appendix B of this manual. In Appendix B the quantity, percent transmittance (%T), is described as a relationship between the intensity of light before and after passing through a solution. Another quantity known as absorbance (A) is related to %T by the following equation:

$$A = \log(100/\%T)$$

The absorbance is related to concentration of a light-absorbing species by the Beer–Lambert Law, $A = \varepsilon bC$, where ε is a proportionality constant called the molar absorptivity that is specific for the absorbing species, **b** is the thickness of the solution in the light path (usually constant for an experiment), and **C** is the molarity of the absorbing species in the solution. For a given light–absorbing species, a plot of absorbance versus concentration should give a straight line. This straight–line relationship can be used to determine the concentration in an unknown solution of the species tested. For this investigation, a plot of the absorbance versus concentration of various cobalt(II) solutions can be used to determine the cobalt (II) ion concentration in the unknown sample sent by the county extension service.

Use the instructions in Appendix B for calibrating the spectrometer or colorimeter. (If neither of these devices is available you can use the non-instrumental technique described in Appendix B.) You will also have to determine the wavelength at which you will run your experiments. A solution of 0.1 *M* cobalt(II) nitrate is available for preparation of your known solutions. (Make sure you write down the exact concentration of the known solution in your lab notebook.) Develop a procedure for using the cobalt(II) nitrate solution to make several dilutions (at least seven). You will have to select an appropriate range of concentrations. Once your solutions are prepared, use the spectrometer or colorimeter to collect absorbance data for each concentration. If a graphing program is readily available, construct a plot of your data that you can use to determine the concentration in the unknown. At high concentrations (that vary from one chemical species to another) there is deviation from the Beer–Lambert Law. Use your plotted data as a guide for identifying the point at which deviation occurs. If you do not see any deviation from linearity, your concentrations could be in the correct range.

Determine if the amount of cobalt(II) in the soil meets the nutritional needs of the animals. If not, you should calculate the amount of cobalt(II) nitrate that must be added to the soil to reach a level of 0.13 to 0.30 mg of cobalt(II) per kilogram of soil.

Report

As usual you should write your report in customary scientific fashion. Include your recommendations to the cooperative extension service regarding amending soil on the county farms. Remember to include appropriate graphs with your report. (Further information about cobalt deficiency can be found by doing an Internet search on the term *cobalt deficiency*.)

Caution:
While working in the laboratory wear your goggles at all times.

How Much Cobalt Is in the Soil? **Team Contribution Form**

Identify the percent contribution each team member made in this investigation, listing your name first.

Name: Percent Contribution:

_____   _____

_____   _____

_____   _____

_____   _____

Describe your contribution to the completion of the investigation and the writing of the report.

Return this sheet to your lab instructor.

Introduction

A company that mines platinum has recently discovered a rich source of copper near one of its mines. The company has asked your savvy chemical team to probe the chemistry of copper and some of its compounds. By understanding the chemistry of copper it hopes that it can easily separate the copper from platinum and other precious metals it mines. Specifically, the company thinks that by starting with copper metal and making copper(II) hydroxide, copper(II) nitrate, and copper(II) sulfate (not necessarily in that order) in some sequence of steps, copper metal can be recovered. If your cyclic synthetic route is successful, the company believes that it can separate the precious metals from the copper during one or more of the steps.

Your team must devise a synthetic route that is cyclic, allowing you to study a series of reactions that ultimately recovers the used copper. The company does not have a chemist on staff so there is not a qualified person available to explain the chemical processes that occur in the production of the copper compounds. The company insists that your report include a careful description of the reaction types that occur as you synthesize the compounds of interest.

Goals

As you complete this investigation you will:
1. Probe the chemical behavior of copper.
2. Synthesize various copper compounds and describe the chemical reactions taking place.
3. Recover the copper metal from the series of reactions that produces the chemicals of interest.
4. Report your findings to the mining company as directed by your instructor.

Materials

Acetone	Zinc
Copper wire	Büchner funnel
3 M HCl(aq)	Litmus paper
6 M HNO$_3$(aq)	Filter flask
6 M NaOH(aq)	Other supplies by request
2 M H$_2$SO$_4$(aq)	

Getting Started

Develop procedures for synthesizing the compounds of interest in a cyclic manner. Solubility rules and a metal activity series might be useful. You should prepare the materials using small quantities of starting material to reduce the amount of waste and to minimize the costs (raw

---

material and waste disposal) to the customer. In addition to your syntheses, you must include a route to recovering native copper which can be returned to the company. Upon completion of a proposal you must obtain your instructor's approval before carrying out experimentation.

You should begin by dissolving a piece of copper metal (not to exceed 0.5 g to conserve the metal) in a suitable amount of nitric acid as directed by your instructor. Alternatively, your instructor might ask you to calculate the amount of nitric acid needed from stoichiometric relationships. You may have to add additional reagent to force the reaction to completion. Careful heating will also help dissolve the copper metal. **Be very careful; you are working with strong acids and bases. In addition, the reaction of copper metal with nitric acid produces toxic NO_2 gas. This reaction should be run in a hood.** The products of this reaction are copper(II) nitrate, nitrogen dioxide, and water. For all the reactions, add the reagents slowly with continuous stirring between additions. As the reactions proceed, make as many observations about the chemical behavior as possible, identifying all products formed. Consider other comments listed below:

- Some products may not be formed as a solid. How can products in solution be isolated?
- When you prepare copper(II) hydroxide *be careful* when adding sodium hydroxide. You should add this reagent *slowly* until the solution just turns basic. If you add the hydroxide too fast you will form black copper(II) oxide instead of copper(II) hydroxide.
- The hydrochloric acid listed previously is available only to remove excess zinc that might be present if you use it as one of your reagents. The HCl reacts with the zinc to form hydrogen gas and zinc chloride. After addition of the HCl you should heat the mixture slightly to make sure all the hydrogen gas has been driven off. **Be very careful** — the hydrogen could ignite if brought too close to the heat source.
- At the end of your experimentation you should have recovered all the copper. You can use a Büchner funnel with a filter flask or another technique to dry your copper. After drying, wash the copper with a little acetone. **Acetone is flammable** so be careful! You should compare your final amount of copper to the amount of starting material by calculating the percent recovered. For each trial compare the percent recovery.

Report

Report your results as directed by your instructor. Your report to the customer should include careful analyses of the reactions you ran. For each synthesis describe the reaction type, write chemical equations, and explain your observations from a microscopic standpoint. Where appropriate, you should write molecular, ionic, and net ionic equations.

> **Caution:**
> While working in the laboratory wear your goggles at all times.
> You are working with strong acids and bases that can damage
> skin and eyes. You are preparing gases that may be flammable
> or toxic, so all reactions should be run in a fume hood.

What Is a Copper Cycle? **Team Contribution Form**

Identify the percent contribution each team member made in this investigation, listing your name first.

Name: Percent Contribution:

_____   _____

_____   _____

_____   _____

_____   _____

Describe your contribution to the completion of the investigation and the writing of the report.

Return this sheet to your lab instructor.

Investigation 8
What's in the Bottles?

Introduction

Among the basic problems which frequently confront a chemist is the analysis of materials to determine both the identity of the elements or groups of elements present in a given substance (*qualitative analysis*) and how much of each is present (*quantitative analysis*). In this investigation, we will focus only on the identification of substances. Chemists often must depend on the observation of the chemical properties of substances in order to make an identification, just as a detective often must depend on the observation of the behavior of individuals suspected of being involved in a crime. The chemist may look for clues concerning the identity of a substance by observations of pH, color, odor, viscosity, and the results of mixing two substances. Typical results might be evolution or absorption of heat, formation of an insoluble solid (*precipitate*), color of the precipitate, evolution of a gas, odor of the gas, and so on.

Suppose your team of chemical investigators is working for an environmental agency. You have been asked to identify the contents of several unlabeled bottles collected in the laboratory of a company that is not complying with standards of correctly labeling chemical supplies. The environmental agency wants your team to determine the contents of each bottle obtained from the laboratory and report your findings.

Goals

As you complete this investigation you will:
1. Observe chemical reactions arising from the mixing of solutions of different chemicals.
2. Use your observations to identify the contents of unlabeled bottles, based on the type of chemical reactions expected.
3. Recognize various classes of chemical reactions.
4. Report your findings as directed by your instructor.

Materials

Set 1: $AgNO_3(aq)$, $Mn(NO_3)_2(aq)$, $Ba(NO_3)_2(aq)$, $HCl(aq)$, $NaOH(aq)$

Set 2: $Zn(NO_3)_2(aq)$, $Al(NO_3)_3(aq)$, $AgNO_3(aq)$, $NaOH(aq)$, $NH_3(aq)$

Set 3: $AgNO_3(aq)$, $Ba(NO_3)_2(aq)$, $HCl(aq)$, $H_2SO_4(aq)$, $NaOH(aq)$

Set 4: $AgNO_3(aq)$, $Pb(NO_3)_2(aq)$, $HCl(aq)$, $NH_3(aq)$, $H_2O(l)$

Litmus paper, universal indicator, or pH meter
Spot-plate
Droppers
Thermometer or temperature probe
Other supplies by request

Getting Started

The purpose of the experiment is to identify the contents of each bottle, matching the bottle numbers or letters with the chemical species listed for your set. You will be assigned one of the four sets of unlabeled bottles previously listed. The sets might be given a unique letter, number, or color code. The bottles will be identified only by codes assigned by the environmental firm. Your first task might be to identify the particular set you have been assigned. Because the environmental firm has limited resources, the only reagents you have available are the contents of the unlabeled bottles. However, you can make observations of the interactions among the contents of the bottles by mixing them with one another in drop-by-drop quantities. From an analysis of the observed results of interaction between the bottle contents, you should be able to identify each solution. If you feel that you need some external reagent to confirm your conclusions, consult your instructor and obtain permission first.

Keep in mind that all the unknown substances listed above dissociate in water. For example, when solid silver nitrate, $AgNO_3$, dissolves in water it produces Ag^+ and NO_3^- ions. However, some substances do not dissociate in water. You might consult a table of solubility rules in your text to determine which combinations of substances will give a solid precipitate.

You might consider using litmus paper to determine if your solutions are acids or bases. Defined simply, an acid is a substance that donates H^+ ions to solution when the substance is in water. A base is a substance that accepts H^+ ions. Chemists use pH as a measure of the acidity or basicity of a substance. A neutral solution has a pH of 7, an acid has a pH below 7, and a base has a pH above 7. You can use red and blue litmus paper to provide a simple qualitative way of determining if a solution is an acid or a base. Red litmus paper will turn blue in the presence of base and blue litmus paper will turn red in the presence of acid. If needed, consult your text for further information regarding acids and bases.

Report

The report must be typed and grammatically correct. It may be returned to you for corrections if it is not acceptable. Keep in mind the context for which you are completing this investigation. Discuss how you determined the identity of the contents in each bottle. A discussion of the chemical reactions you observed and equations that represent those reactions must be embedded in an appropriate section of your report. You should also identify each chemical reaction according to its reaction class (single displacement, double displacement, and so on). Also, write net ionic equations and identify spectator ions when appropriate.

Caution:
While working in the laboratory wear your goggles at all times.
You are working with strong acids and bases that can cause
permanent damage to eyes and skin.

What's in the Bottles? **Team Contribution Form**

Identify the percent contribution each team member made in this investigation, listing your name first.

Name: Percent Contribution:

_____   _____

_____   _____

_____   _____

_____   _____

Describe your contribution to the completion of the investigation and the writing of the report.

Return this sheet to your lab instructor.

Introduction

All physical and chemical processes are accompanied by changes in energy, often in the form of heat. For example, when a substance cools it loses heat to the environment. Changes in energy are guided by the *first law of thermodynamics*, which states that the energy of the universe is constant. You will use this law to solve the problem posed in this investigation.

Suppose you have recently been put on a technical service team to help your company's customers with your product line. One customer recently returned the coffee pot you manufacture, claiming that the temperature of the water is not hot enough to brew coffee. Your team must measure the temperature of the water inside the pot. Unfortunately, the only thermometer you have available to you has no marks above 40°C. Using only this thermometer and other materials in your lab (except another thermometer), devise and carry out methods to determine the temperature of the water inside the pot.

Goals

As you complete this investigation you will:
1. Apply the principles of thermochemistry to solve your company's problem.
2. Design two alternative approaches to solving the problem.
3. Report your results as directed by your instructor.

Materials

Coffeepot
40°C thermometer
Styrofoam cups
Stirrers
Graduated cylinders, burets, pipets, or other volume measuring devices
Balances
Ice
Cold water
Samples of various metals
Other supplies by request

Getting Started

You may need to consult your textbook about heat transfer, specific heat, and the first law of thermodynamics. Design an experiment that will allow you to determine the temperature of the water in the pot with the 40°C thermometer. You may do anything you wish to bring the water temperature into the range of the thermometer, provided that the measurements you take can be used to calculate the original temperature of the coffeepot water. When you collect your hot water samples, make sure the coffee pot has been on long enough for them to be at its highest temperature. Consider precautions that you might take to prevent the water from cooling off before you start your procedure. Run several trials to confirm the validity of your technique and the data you obtain. Devise a second method for determining the temperature of the water.

Report

Submit a report written in the usual scientific fashion. It may be returned to you for corrections if it is not acceptable. In addition to describing your methods and results, describe your group's alternative approach to solving the problem and the data you expect to obtain from that approach.

Caution:
While working in the laboratory wear your goggles at all times.
Be careful handling the hot water to avoid burns.

How Hot Is the Water? **Team Contribution Report Form**

Identify the percent contribution each team member made in this investigation, listing your name first.

Name: Percent Contribution:

_____   _____

_____   _____

_____   _____

_____   _____

Describe your contribution to the completion of this investigation and the writing of the report.

Return this sheet to your lab instructor.

Introduction

When chemists use materials in various processes, such as the synthesis of new substances, it is convenient to use pure materials. However, the purification of materials, whether by physical or chemical methods, is often quite expensive. Sometimes it is much cheaper to use materials that contain impurities; that is, the material might be a mixture of two or more substances. If substances with impurities are to be used in a chemical process, however, it is necessary to know how much of each substance is present in the mixture. Determining the amount of each substance in a mixture is often carried out by chemical means.

A chemical manufacturing company that uses sodium bicarbonate as a precursor to other sodium compounds recently contracted for your team's services to determine the amount of sodium bicarbonate in a mixture known to contain sodium chloride. It wants to know if this is a reasonable mixture for sodium carbonate production. If the mixture contains more than 90% sodium bicarbonate, then the reduced purity of their product is worth the savings on raw material. Using the materials available in your facility you are to devise and carry out methods for determining the relative amounts of each substance in the mixture and report your findings to the manufacturing company.

Goals

As you complete this investigation you will:
1. Devise two or more methods to determine the percent composition of a mixture.
2. Carry out multiple trials of one such method and determine the amounts of $NaHCO_3$ and NaCl in a mixture containing only these two substances.
3. Report your findings to the chemical manufacturing company as directed by your instructor.

Materials

Sodium chloride, pure
Sodium bicarbonate, pure
Unknown mixture of sodium chloride and sodium bicarbonate
1 *M* hydrochloric acid
1 *M* sulfuric acid
1 *M* sodium hydroxide
Balances and other common laboratory equipment
Other supplies by request

Getting Started

You will be given a white powder, which is a mixture of two solids: sodium bicarbonate ($NaHCO_3$) and sodium chloride ($NaCl$). You are to determine the percentages by mass of each solid in the mixture. Devise at least two chemical procedures for determining the composition of the mixture. Select the one you think has the greatest chance of success and try it out on the pure substances, and on a mixture that you make from the pure substances.

Using the reagents provided, you might begin by studying the chemical properties of the pure substances present in the mixture. Note that the solutions provided are not standardized. This may impact the procedure your group devises. As you design your experiments, how will you know when the reactions come to completion? If you decide to add reagents to the mixture, how will you know how much to add? **Warning: You are working with strong acids and bases that are dangerous to skin and eyes. Rinse thoroughly if any acid or base gets on your skin or in your eyes.** Consult your textbook or other resources about the chemical behavior of the mixture components. Apply your method to the unknown. If time permits and if directed by your instructor, try the alternative method your group designed.

Report

Submit a report as directed by your instructor. Describe the method you used and report the results on the percent composition to a number of significant figures that is suitable for the data that you collected. Also, describe an alternative method for determining the mixture composition. Compare your results to those other teams obtained. Based on your results, what recommendation will you make to the chemical manufacturing company? If directed to do so by your instructor, consult information on the Internet to compare prices of sodium bicarbonate at various purities.

Caution:
While working in the laboratory wear your goggles at all times.
You are working with strong acids and bases that can cause
damage to skin and eyes.

How Much Sodium Bicarbonate Is in the Mixture? **Team Contribution Form**

Identify the percent contribution each team member made in this investigation, listing your name first.

Name: Percent Contribution:

_____   _____

_____   _____

_____   _____

_____   _____

Describe your contribution to the completion of the investigation and the writing of the report.

Return this sheet to your lab instructor.

Investigation 11
What Is the pH of Soil?

Introduction

The acidity of soils is very important in the growing of foodstuffs. The pH of the soil is a factor in regulating the availability of plant nutrients and the activity of soil bacteria. In some cases, controlled acidity may help prevent growth of weeds and certain destructive insects. Some plants grow well only in slightly acid soils while excess acidity may prevent good growth with other plants. In alkaline soils (pH > 8), such as are found in desert regions, the amounts of nitrogen, phosphorus, iron, and other nutrients are too low for good plant growth and special procedures such as neutralization by acid treatment must be carried out to make the soil suitable for agriculture. The County Agricultural Extension Service wants you to determine the pH of some soil samples and the effect of various additives on the pH of these soils.

Goals

As you complete this investigation you will:
1. Develop a method for measuring whether a soil is acidic, basic, or neutral.
2. Use your method to determine the pH of some soil samples.
3. Add some fertilizer components to soil samples to make mixtures that are as homogeneous as possible. Measure the effect of these components on the pH of the soil samples.
4. Report your findings as directed by your instructor.

Materials

Soil samples
Soil additives:

> Lime, $Ca(OH)_2$
> Iron(III) sulfate, $Fe_2(SO_4)_3$
> Ammonium sulfate, $(NH_4)_2SO_4$
> Potassium chloride, KCl
> Diammonium hydrogen phosphate, $(NH_4)_2HPO_4$

Red litmus paper (turns blue when wet with a basic solution)
Blue litmus paper (turns red when wet with an acidic solution)
Bromcresol purple solution (yellow if pH < 5.2 and purple if pH > 6.8; green between these pH values)
Distilled water
Glass plate or spot plate
Spatula
Glass rod
Other supplies by request

Getting Started

Begin by developing a method for determining the acidity of a known soil. Use the two acid-base indicators, litmus and bromcresol purple. A pH meter could also be used if one is available. (See Appendix C for more information about pH.) Your glassware must be very clean or it might cause a change of pH. How can you check this? When you have checked your method on a soil sample of know pH, use it to determine the acidity of the unknown soils. Then, one at a time, add the various soil additives to different soil samples. Do this in such a way as to make the mixture as homogeneous as possible. What quantities will you use? Use your method to determine the effect of these additives on the acidity of the soil.

Report

Submit a report to the Extension Service that describes the method you developed for measuring acidity. Include the results for the various soil samples. Describe the effect on pH of the various soil additives. Also include a description of why these soil additives might be used to assist plant growth.

+--+
| **Caution:** |
| **Wear your goggles at all times.** |
+--+

What Is the pH of Soil? **Team Contribution Form**

Identify the percent contribution each team member made in this investigation listing your name first.

Group: Percent Contribution:

_____   _____

_____   _____

_____   _____

_____   _____

Describe your contribution to the completion of the investigation and the writing of the report.

Return this sheet to your lab instructor.

Investigation 12
How Can a Battery Be Made from Coins?

Introduction

In 1800 Alessandro Volta created the first battery, which consisted of alternating layers of zinc, paper soaked in salt water, and silver. This battery has come to be known as a voltaic pile. Your group can create your own pile by using coins and paper towels. Suppose your group was stranded on a boat somewhere in the ocean and you have to power up your GPS (global positioning system). You have no replacement batteries but you have a pocket full of coins. How much voltage can you generate from these coins to make a battery?

Goals

As you complete this investigation you will:
1. Develop a procedure for measuring the voltage of a pile of coins.
2. Vary the coin composition and arrangement.
3. Report your findings as directed by your instructor.

Materials

Coins (bring your own)   A device for measuring voltage
NaCl(s)   Acetic acid and/or steel wool to clean the coins
Filter paper or paper toweling

Getting Started

You might begin by constructing a voltaic pile consisting of pennies and dimes. Try starting with a saturated solution of sodium chloride for soaking the paper. Alternate layers of pennies, paper soaked in salt water, and dimes. The coins should be cleaned with some acetic acid and/or steel wool before you begin. Measure the voltage of the pile. Does the voltage vary with pile height? If so, does it vary consistently with additional layers? From your saturated NaCl solution, prepare other concentrations. How does the voltage vary with different concentrations of salt water? How does the voltage vary with different types of coins? Consult Appendix F for instructions about measuring voltage with your equipment.

Report

The report must be typed and grammatically correct. It may be returned to you for corrections if it is not acceptable. Include a thorough discussion of your observations, answering the questions posed in this investigation.

```
Caution:
Wear your goggles at all times.
```

How Can a Battery Be Made from Coins? Team Contribution Form

Identify the percent contribution each team member made in this investigation, listing your name first.

Name: Percent Contribution:

_____   _____

_____   _____

_____   _____

_____   _____

Describe your contribution to the completion of this investigation and the writing of the report.

Return this sheet to your lab instructor.

Investigation 13
Who Wrote the Ransom Note?

Introduction

Criminal investigators use chemistry routinely to solve crimes. One important technique in a forensics lab, *chromatography*, involves the separation of mixtures found in evidence at a crime scene. For example, sometimes a piece of evidence might be an ink sample. Forgery cases, kidnapping cases (involving a ransom note), and other crimes involving writing are often investigated using an analytical tool called chromatography. Chromatography is a general term referring to the separation of a mixture. In this investigation, your team will be given a sample of ink found at the scene of a crime. Your job will be to determine which pen made the ink mark.

Goals

As you complete this investigation, you will:
1. Learn about the technique of paper chromatography.
2. Develop a paper chromatography technique to separate components in an ink sample.
3. Identify an ink sample based on its chromatogram.
4. Write a report that could be used as evidence in a criminal trial.

Materials

Black ink pens	Plastic wrap or beaker cover
Chromatography paper	Ink sample from "crime scene"
Scissors	Deionized water
Large beaker	20%, 50%, and 90% ethanol solutions
Rulers	Other supplies by request

Getting Started

Paper chromatography is one type of chromatography used to separate a mixture of components (such as ink) to observe its component substances. Black ink is usually a mixture of several different colors that can be separated under appropriate chromatographic conditions. Inks from different pens are commonly composed of different components that make the ink unique. To separate the components in an ink sample, a small dot of ink is placed on a strip of chromatography paper about 2.5 cm from the end. The paper is then stood up in a beaker containing about 1 to 1.5 cm of solvent. The chromatography paper soaks up the solvent slowly and the ink migrates with it towards the top of the paper. The individual components of the ink move at different rates and a pattern characteristic of the ink appears on the paper. Why should the solvent depth remain below the level of the ink dots?

Designing chromatography experiments usually involves selection of the proper solvent for the system of interest. In this investigation your team of crime specialists has been provided several solutions of ethanol with water. Your first task should be to determine which solvent mixture is appropriate for separation of ink components in the known pens. In addition to the ethanol solutions, you should try using water as the solvent. Why do you suppose some solvent systems work better than others?

Your group will be given one or two samples of ink taken from a crime scene. Because the sample is taken from a limited supply that will be used in court, do not use the unknown until your team is certain of the solvent system you will use.

In addition to determining the proper solvent, you should develop a way of quantifying your data for your report; that is, you might consider ways of expressing your results in numerical terms that allow for easy comparison of results from one experiment to another.

Report

The report must be typed, grammatically correct, and suitable for presentation in a court of law. It may be returned to you for corrections if it is not acceptable. Your report should include a discussion of factors that may affect the rate at which the solvent and the ink components move up the chromatography paper. Remember that your report may be used in a court of law. If directed by your instructor, include your chromatograms with your report.

Caution:
While working in the laboratory wear your goggles at all times.
You are working with solvents that may be flammable.

Who Wrote the Ransom Note? Team Contribution Form

Identify the percent contribution each team member made in this investigation, listing your name first.

Name: Percent Contribution:

_____   _____

_____   _____

_____   _____

_____   _____

Describe your contribution to the completion of the investigation and the writing of the report.

Return this sheet to your lab instructor.

Investigation 14
What Factors Affect Chemical Equilibrium?

Introduction

Addition of a solution of NH$_4$NCS to a solution of Fe(NO$_3$)$_3$ results in a blood-red color. The more NH$_4$NCS added, the more intense the red color. Aqueous Fe^{3+} and NCS$^-$ combine to form a complex ion in an equilibrium reaction:

$$Fe^{3+}(aq) + NCS^-(aq) \rightleftharpoons FeNCS^{2+}(aq)$$

There are many factors that can change the position of the equilibrium once the reaction appears to have stopped. In this investigation you will identify factors that have an effect on the above reaction.

Goals

As you complete this investigation you will:
1. Observe what happens when various substances are added to an equilibrium mixture.
2. Describe the chemistry taking place when reagents are added that change the equilibrium system.
3. Explain why the equilibrium position changes when the mixture is heated and cooled.
4. Identify patterns about stresses placed on equilibrium systems.
5. Summarize your findings in a written report as directed by your instructor.

Materials

1 M Fe(NO$_3$)$_3$(aq)   1M NH$_3$(aq)
1 M NH$_4$NCS(aq)   Bunsen burner
0.10 M SnCl$_2$(aq)   Ice
0.1 M AgNO$_3$(aq)   Other supplies by request
1 M Na$_2$HPO$_4$(aq)

Getting Started

You should begin by observing the formation of the iron thiocyanate by placing 8 drops of 1 M Fe(NO$_3$)$_3$ and 8 drops of 1 M NH$_4$NCS in 100 mL of water. You should design an experiment that will test the effects on the equilibrium when other reagents are added to the system. Your design must minimize reagent use; that is, when placing the external stresses on the equilibrium

---

you should observe what happens when reagents are added in a drop–by–drop fashion. Upon addition of each reagent identify other chemical reactions that might be occurring. Do any patterns emerge about the direction in which the equilibrium shifts when particular reagents are added?

In addition to chemical stresses, observe what happens when the equilibrium system is heated (but not to boiling) and cooled. What conclusions can you draw about the exo- or endothermicity of the reaction?

Report

Report your findings as directed by your instructor. Your report should include a discussion of pertinent chemical reactions and observations.

> **Caution:**
> **Wear your goggles at all times. You are working with a strong base that can damage skin and eyes. Avoid inhaling the ammonia fumes. Silver nitrate can stain skin and clothing.**

What Factors Affect Chemical Equilibrium? **Team Contribution Form**

Identify the percent contribution each team member made in this investigation, listing your name first.

Name: Percent Contribution:

_____   _____

_____   _____

_____   _____

_____   _____

Describe your contribution to the investigation and the writing of the report.

Return this sheet to your lab instructor.

Investigation 15
What Formulation Makes the Best Toy?

Introduction

A toy manufacturer wishes to break into a specialized toy market that depends on various properties of polymers. Using a combination of glue and sodium borate they believe that a slime-type of polymer using polyvinyl acetate can be developed. They hope this unique product can be packaged and sold in toy stores. The company wants your group to produce several variations of glue/sodium borate combinations and compare their properties. The group that can produce a ball with the best bounce will win the company's contract.

Goals

As you complete this investigation you will:
1. Develop formations of polymers containing polyvinyl acetate.
2. Compare viscosity properties of the different formulations.
3. Develop a combination of raw materials that produce a final product that will bounce.
4. Report findings to the toy manufacturer as directed by your instructor.

Materials

White glue (polyvinyl acetate)
Sodium borate
Balances
Graduated cylinder, burets, pipets, or other volume measuring devices
Hot plates
Other supplies by request

Getting Started

In this investigation you will prepare several different products that contain various amounts of polyvinyl acetate, water and sodium borate. By varying the ratios of these starting materials, properties such as viscosity might change. Because of the complexity of the reaction taking place, you cannot merely add water and solid sodium borate to glue. Instead, some glue has to be mixed with water, the sodium borate has to be dissolved in water, and the two solutions combined. You should begin your first formulation using a 1:1:1:1 mass ratio of each component – 10 gram quantities should suffice. Start by dissolving 10 g glue in 10 g of distilled water. (Assume a density of 1 g/mL for distilled water.) Also dissolve 10 g of sodium borate in 10 g of distilled water. The two solutions can be mixed by adding the glue mixture to the sodium borate solution. You may have to work the mixture with your hands to thoroughly mix the components.

When you prepare variations of the 1:1:1:1 ratio of glue/water/sodium borate/water, you should keep the total mass constant. Develop a technique for comparing the viscosity and bouncability of each formulation.

Report

The report must be typed and grammatically correct. It may be returned to you for corrections if it is not acceptable. Include your recommendations to the toy manufacturer.

> **Caution:**
> **Wear your goggles at all times. Sodium borate is lightly toxic if inhaled or ingested. Some people are allergic to soaps containing sodium borate so wash your hands frequently during this investigation.**

What Formulation Makes the Best Toy? **Team Contribution Form**

Identify the percent contribution each team member made in this investigation, listing your name first.

Name: Percent Contribution:

_____   _____

_____   _____

_____   _____

_____   _____

Describe your contribution to the completion of the investigation and the writing of the report.

Return this sheet to your lab instructor.

	Investigation 16	
	How Can We Identify the Unknown Plastic?	

Introduction

Different plastics are composed of different polymers that give each plastic unique properties. For proper recycling, the type of plastic must be identified. Many containers and other plastics are labeled with classification codes. However, this is done on a voluntary basis by the plastic manufacturer, and this information is not always available. A large shipment of unlabeled mixed plastics has recently been delivered to a local recycling facility. Your team has been hired to identify the different types of plastics so that they can be separated and recycled appropriately.

Goals

As you complete this investigation you will:
1. Determine the density of different types of plastic.
2. Observe the results of the melting of different types of plastics.
3. Observe the results of the burning of different types of plastics.
4. Identify the unknown plastics based on their physical properties.
5. Report your findings as directed by your instructor.

Materials

Strips of various types of plastics
0.1 M NaCl solution (density = 1.08 g/mL)
95% Ethanol solution (density = 0.94 g/mL)
Distilled water (density = 1.0 g/mL)
Heat source
Flame source
Test tubes
Spatulas
Volumetric glassware

Getting Started

The purpose of this experiment is to identify the type of plastic in each strip. Plastics are made of *polymers*, large chains of molecules of varying lengths that are covalently linked to each other. The smaller molecules used to synthesize polymers are called *monomers*. There are six major groups of recyclable plastics: polyethylene terphthalate (PET or PETE), high-density polyethylene (HDPE), polyvinyl chloride (V), low-density polyethylene (LDPE), polypropylene (PP), and polystyrene (PS). Each of these plastics fall under the category of *thermoplastics*, polymers that can be melted and shaped, and when cooled retain there chemical composition. The physical properties of each type of plastic varies. Some are brittle, some are hard, some are flexible, and some are rigid. Each type of plastic also has distinct characteristics when heated and burned, and each type of plastic has a distinct density. These properties can be used to identify the type of plastic in a given sample.

Table 1: Densities for various plastics

	PETE	HDPE	V	LDPE	PP	PS
Density (g/mL)	1.38-1.39	0.95-0.97	1.18-1.65	0.92-0.94	0.90-0.91	1.05-1.07

Report

The report must be typed and grammatically correct. It may be returned to you for corrections if it is not acceptable. Keep in mind the context for which you are completing this investigation. Discuss how you determined the identity of each of the plastics. A discussion of the observations made during the experiment must be included in the appropriate section of your report

> **Caution:**
> **While working in the laboratory wear your goggles at all times.**
> **Plastics release toxic gases when burned. ALL burning**
> **experiments must be performed in the ventilation hood.**

How Can We Identify the Unknown Plastic? **Team Contribution Form**

Identify the percent contribution each team member made in this investigation, listing your name first.

Name: Percent Contribution:

_____   _____

_____   _____

_____   _____

_____   _____

Describe your contribution to the completion of the investigation and the writing of the report.

Return this sheet to your lab instructor.

Presentations and Poster Sessions

At the end of the semester all students are expected to present the findings of an investigation in two forms: an oral presentation to your fellow class members and on a large poster board. At the beginning of the lab period your group will do a ten–minute presentation that summarizes your findings. The exposition need not be of a formal scientific type — feel free to pursue a more creative avenue for your presentation. Regardless of your presentation format, you must summarize your experiment and results in some way. You might consult some of the resources on the Internet that offer suggestions for giving a good presentation.

Scientists often present their work at scientific meetings in the form of poster sessions. The poster typically summarizes the investigation in words, graphs, tables, and figures. Your instructor might direct you to examples scattered around your campus. The posted should be organized, visually appealing, easy to read from a distance, and summarize your experiment.

The poster session will be held immediately after your class's presentations. You are expected to wander by your fellow students' posters in your class and in other sections. In 15 minute shifts, your group members will take turns standing by your poster to field questions from people who are interested in your work. Someone should be near your poster at all times. Expect your fellow students, your instructor, and other guests to ask you questions about your experimental methods and results. You should also ask questions of the other groups as you browse their work.

Your instructor will grade your presentation and poster according to the following criteria:

- Your group's ability to convey an understanding of the investigation during the presentation.
- Your group's presentation skills.
- The creativity of your presentation.
- The scientific accuracy of your findings.
- Your poster's ability to convey an adequate representation of the experiment.
- Proper use of tables, diagrams, and graphs where appropriate.
- The organization and clarity of your poster.
- Your ability to field questions from people browsing through the posters.

Your poster must be visually appealing. Some students make the mistake of merely pasting their lab reports onto a piece of poster board. Also, your reader must be able to see the text from some distance away from the poster.

Presentation/Poster Session Team Contribution Report Form

Identify the percent contribution each team member made to the *presentation*, listing your name first.

Name: Percent Contribution:

_____   _____

_____   _____

_____   _____

_____   _____

Describe your contribution to the *presentation*.

Identify the percent contribution each team member made to the preparation of the *poster*, listing your name first.

Name: Percent Contribution:

_____   _____

_____   _____

_____   _____

_____   _____

Describe your contribution to the *poster*.

Automated Data Collection

Your lab may be equipped with automated data collection devices. These are typically calculator based (CBL) or microcomputer based (MBL). Some devices can even be operated with a personal data assistant (PDA). The CBL and PDA systems are more portable than the MBL system. The MBL system is directly connected to the computer so the data can be manipulated without additional data transfer steps.

Automated data collection involves a device used as an interface between a *probe* and a computer, calculator, or PDA. The CBL, the LabPro, and the LabQuest are all examples of interface devices. There are many types of probes that can measure temperature, color intensity (absorbance), pressure, voltage, pH, and other properties.

LabPro
Photograph Courtesy of
Vernier Software & Technology

Many automated data collection systems are microcomputer-based. The interface is connected directly to a computer. Data from the probe is stored directly in the computer via the interface. The LabPro and LabQuest systems (from Vernier) are examples of interfaces that can be connected directly to a computer.

Specific instructions for your device will be provided by your instructor. Generally, when using automated data collection one must:

    a) Connect the probe(s), interface, and computer (or calculator) correctly.
    b) Specify the probe identity to the computer.
    c) Choose the data collection mode.

The system will likely be capable of several different collection modes. Your experiment may require you to collect data manually (e.g. record the pH after the addition of base). You may want to collect data at regular time intervals (e.g. record the pH every 20 seconds for 10 minutes). Learn how to use the different collection modes available to you. Automated data collection and record keeping are very valuable tools in the chemical laboratory.

Calibration is necessary for some probes. Colorimeters and pH probes should always be calibrated immediately before use. Some probes are pre-calibrated. These pre-calibrated probes will usually be recognized by the computer and a stored calibration will automatically be incorporated.

After the data is collected, it may need to be transferred to a computer program of choice, and it will need to be treated for proper display for your lab report. If the data is collected with a calculator-based system, then it will need to be uploaded to a computer for adequate treatment and to ensure the printout will be professional in quality. Learn the necessary steps for getting your data into a computer with the equipment available. Microcomputer based systems will already have the data stored in the computer. Often the data is stored in a program that will manipulate the data adequately for your laboratory investigations. Many students prefer to transfer the data from the default program into a graphing software they are more comfortable with. This is usually as simple as copying the data from the default spreadsheet, opening the program of choice, and then pasting the data into the spreadsheet within. See Appendix G for more information about graphing and data processing in the laboratory.

Electronic copies of your data and graphs should always be saved to ensure they are available in case you need to modify your report.

Transmittance and Absorbance Data Collection

Introduction

Spectroscopy is the chemical discipline that studies the interaction of electromagnetic radiation with matter. In a typical spectroscopy experiment, the item to be analyzed is placed in a chamber, then exposed to some form of electromagnetic radiation. The sample will absorb radiation at some wavelengths and other wavelengths will pass through. Spectroscopy offers many techniques that help scientists characterize substances qualitatively (identification of the species present in a material) and quantitatively (the amount of each species present). While some chemical techniques for identifying substances are destructive to the system under investigation, spectroscopic techniques are typically nondestructive to the sample of interest. The power of spectroscopy rests on the specific behavior of substances when exposed to light. For example, a certain solution will have color because light is absorbed at some wavelengths, but not at others. When light is passed through a solution, the light arrives at the wall of the container (for example, a cuvette) with some intensity, I_o. Some of the light is absorbed as it passes through the solution, so the intensity of light leaving the solution, I is less than the initial intensity. The ratio of intensities, converted to a percentage, is called the % transmittance (%T):

$$\%T = I/I_o \times 100$$

Transmittance is used to quantify the relationship between the intensity of the radiation passing through the sample (I), and the intensity of the radiation to which the sample was exposed (I_0): specifically, transmittance is the ratio of the two:

$$T = I/I_0$$

Or, expressed as a percentage as it often is:

$$\%T = I/I_0 \times 100$$

When you conduct spectroscopy experiments with a spectrophotometer or colorimeter, one of the critical design issues is selection of the proper wavelength to which your sample will be exposed; that is, the light transmitted through a solution depends on the wavelengths that are absorbed by the solution components.

A detector is used to measure the intensity of the radiation passing through the sample. The detector is calibrated prior to measuring the %T of the sample. Typically the calibration is achieved by assigning deionized water (or another solvent) a value of 100%T. Additionally, the detector is blocked so that no radiation can enter, and a value of 0%T is assigned.

In addition to collecting transmittance data as described above, you can collect absorbance data. Absorbance is a measure of the amount of light absorbed by a sample. Typically a spectrometer will be capable of displaying both %T and absorbance values. The specific mathematical relationship between %T and absorbance is not shown here since it is presented as an exercise in *What Factors Affect the Intensity of Color?*.

This appendix describes the collection of absorbance (A) and percent transmittance (%T) data.

Transmittance and Absorbance Data Collection

When collecting absorbance or transmittance data, three steps will be involved:

    a) Determining the proper wavelength of light for the sample.
    b) Calibrating the spectrophotometer (or colorimeter) with an appropriate "blank".
    c) Measuring the absorbance (or transmittance) of the sample(s).

Selecting the proper wavelength could be an interesting investigation by itself. The task is to find the wavelength of light where the sample has a maximum absorbance, or response, to the probe. Some colorimeters have only a few wavelengths of light available. With these types of colorimeters, a sample's absorbance could be compared to a "blank" at all available wavelengths, and the wavelength showing the maximum absorbance will be the desired wavelength. Some colorimeters have a diffraction grating which allows the user to select any wavelength within the range of the instrument. With these colorimeters, also called spectrophotometers, the user can scan through the range of wavelengths and watch the absorbance change with the varying wavelength. Again, the wavelength showing the maximum absorbance (compared to the blank) will be the desired wavelength.

Vernier Colorimeter
Photograph Courtesy of
Vernier Software & Technology

Calibrating the colorimeter for a particular set of measurements will involve a few important steps. First, if necessary, the instrument must be connected to the proper interface and computer. It needs to be turned on and allowed to warm to its normal operating temperature. Calibration requires a "blank" solution. The "blank" is often deionized water or another appropriate solvent. Your instrument will be calibrated by placing the "blank" in the sample chamber and telling the instrument (or computer) to read this as zero absorbance, or 100% transmittance. The instrument will also have a setting which prevents light from entering the detector. During calibration, this setting will be used and the instrument (or computer) must be told to read this as infinite absorbance, or 0% transmittance. Once the 0% T and 100% T readings have been entered into the instrument (or computer), the colorimeter is calibrated. It is important to note that the instrument can "drift" out of calibration. The calibration settings should be checked and adjusted periodically during any investigation involving the collection of absorbance data. The instrument will need to be re-calibrated if the wavelength of light is changed.

Once the instrument is calibrated, it is ready for absorbance measurements of samples. This will often be as simple as placing the sample in the chamber, closing the cover, and reading the absorbance. If using an automated data collection device, a button or "trigger" may need to be pushed to collect and store the absorbance reading. Most CBL and MBL interfaces will collect both absorbance and percent transmittance. It is important to know which of these is being displayed by the instrument during the collection of data. Most interfaces will allow you to collect data manually or during regular assigned time intervals. Your instructor can help with the specific buttons and capabilities of the colorimeter available to you.

Measuring pH

There are several ways to measure pH. The method you use depends on how accurately you want to know the pH.

Indicators

Colored indicators are often used to measure pH. These indicators are a different color in a basic environment than in an acidic environment. Litmus, for example, is blue in a basic environment and red in an acidic environment. Paper coated with litmus (litmus paper) can be used to determine whether a solution is basic or acidic. Paper coated with Universal Indicator (pH paper) can be dipped into a solution to determine its pH within 1 pH unit. Universal Indicator is a combination of indicators which will produce a different color for each pH value. To use pH paper, just dip the paper into the solution to be measured and then compare the color to the color chart supplied with the paper. To measure the pH of a gas, moisten the pH paper with deionized water and then expose the moistened paper to the gas.

An indicator can be added directly to a solution to determine its pH. The specific pH range corresponding to each color may be supplied with your indicator, or may only be available to you by using a reference book. If you know the pH range at which an indicator changes color, then you can know whether a solution is at that pH, above that pH, or below that pH.

pH Meter

A pH meter consists of two electrodes connected to a voltmeter, which is capable of measuring small differences in electrical potential. A pH meter can often measure pH to within 0.01 pH units. Most manufacturers make combination electrodes which have both electrodes physically located within one tube. One electrode is a reference and the other (indicator electrode) is sensitive to changes in pH. The most common indicator electrode is the glass electrode which contains a solution within a glass bulb having a thin glass membrane. If the solution on the outside of the membrane is of a different pH than the solution within, then an electrical potential will develop across the membrane. This potential difference is measured by the voltmeter. A pH meter will directly convert the voltage into pH units. The meter must be calibrated prior to making pH measurements. A CBL or MBL system equipped with a pH probe can be used as a pH meter and must similarly be calibrated.

pH Meter

This appendix describes the procedure for calibrating and making pH measurements. Directions for use will vary slightly with the model of pH meter used. Consult your instructor or the operator's manual for specific instructions for your pH meter or probe.

General Instructions for pH Measurement

1. Electrodes should always be supported with a clamp when in use. If separate electrodes are used, then they should not be allowed to touch each other or the bottom or sides of the container.

2. Glass electrodes are extremely fragile. Be careful. If the electrode is covered with a guard sleeve, then do not remove this sleeve. Make sure the electrode is immersed far enough to cover the perforation in the sleeve when making measurements.

3. After making a pH measurement, immediately rinse the electrode(s) with deionized water and gently pat dry with a lint-free tissue to prevent contamination of the next solution.

4. When the pH meter is not in use, the electrodes must be soaked in water or a neutral pH buffer solution. If the glass membrane dries out, then the electrode will become inoperative.

5. When calibrating the pH meter, use at least two standard buffer solutions. Ideally, one should have a pH value higher than the solutions to be measured, and the other should have a pH value lower than the solutions to be measured. It is best if the buffers are also close in pH to the solutions of interest.

Taking pH Measurements in the Laboratory

1. Connect the pH probe to the appropriate meter, or interface and computer.

2. Select the appropriate software (if necessary) and identify the probe type (pH).

3. You should always perform new calibrations with the pH probe. When using a pH probe and interface, the software will take you through a two-point calibration procedure for which buffer solutions are needed. When the software prompts you to calibrate point 1, insert the pH probe in the lower pH buffer solution, wait until the voltage reading stabilizes, and import the data (this may require you to push a button or "trigger").*

4. The software will then prompt you for the pH of the buffer solution; input the value to assign the proper pH to the imported data.

5. The calculator will then prompt you for the second reference point. After rinsing the probe in deionized water and patting the tip dry with a soft tissue, insert the probe in the higher pH buffer solution. Again, wait until the voltage reading stabilizes, and import the data (this may require you to push a button or "trigger").

6. Input the pH of the second pH reference solution. You can now collect pH data.

7. Select the desired mode of data collection. Most interfaces will allow you to collect data manually or during regular assigned time intervals. Your instructor can help with the specific buttons and capabilities of the pH system available to you.

8. After rinsing the probe with deionized water and again patting the tip dry with a soft tissue, insert the probe into the solution to be measured and start your manual or automated data collection.

9. When you are finished using the pH probe, rinse it and immerse it in its storage solution.

*A laboratory pH meter is a self-contained instrument that includes a pH probe, interface, voltmeter, and a display or readout. This instrument is typically calibrated by "dialing" the instrument's standardization knob to match the pH's of the buffer solutions. Your instructor can help with the specific buttons and steps required to calibrate your pH meter if one is available to you.

Temperature Data Collection

Temperature can be measured using a thermometer or a temperature probe connected to a CBL or MBL system. The automated systems are particularly useful when a series of temperature measurements are required over the course of an experiment. Some brief instructions for using a temperature probe with the CBL are listed below. The MBL system would probably require less steps than the CBL system, and would have the added advantage of storing your temperature data directly in the computer. For more information about CBL and MBL systems, see Appendix A.

Temperature Measurements with the CBL or MBL

1. Connect the temperature probe to the interface unit and to the calculator (or computer).

2. Select the appropriate software (if necessary) and identify the probe type (temperature). The software may already recognize the probe type without any additional identification.

Because the temperature probe is already calibrated, a calibration menu will probably not appear when you use the temperature probe.

3. Select the desired mode of data collection. Most interfaces will allow you to collect data manually or during regular assigned time intervals. Your instructor can help with the specific buttons and capabilities of the automated data collection system available to you.

Vernier Temperature Probe
Photograph Courtesy of
Vernier Software & Technology

Pressure Data Collection

Pressure changes can be monitored using a pressure sensor connected to an interface and a graphing calculator, or connected to an MBL system. Pressure can also be measured in the laboratory using a simple manometer. This appendix shows some details of taking pressure measurements with a CBL or MBL system, and describes the use of a simple laboratory manometer. Consult your instructor if your equipment differs significantly from that described here.

Pressure Measurements with a Pressure Sensor

1. Prepare the pressure sensor for data collection.

    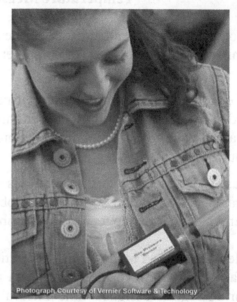

    Figure 1
    Photograph Courtesy of
    Vernier Software & Technology

    • Plug the pressure sensor into the interface and calculator (or computer). A 20-mL syringe or other gas container can be connected to the valve.
    • To allow air or other gases to enter or exit the pressure sensor and container, open the valve to the pressure sensor. Some pressure sensors have a three-way valve. This type valve is used to select which gas sample is to be exposed to the probe. The probe can be open to the room, open to a sample chamber and closed to the room, or closed to both (see Figures 2 and 3). Familiarize yourself with the valve connected to your pressure sensor. Know which position opens the sample to the sensor.

Figure 2

Figure 3

2. Select the appropriate software (if necessary) and identify the probe type (pressure). Note there are several types of pressure probes. These include probes that measure the pressure of all gases, and probes that measure the pressure of specific gases, like O_2. Make sure you identify the correct type of pressure probe.

3. Select the desired mode of data collection. Most interfaces will allow you to collect data manually or during regular assigned time intervals. Your instructor can help with the specific buttons and capabilities of the pressure system available to you.

4. Collect your data. Some pressure sensors only measure pressures up to 1.5 atm. Some laboratory equipment will break or explode when gases are produced or heated in a closed system. Know the limits of your equipment and the pressure probe before designing any investigations involving pressure measurements.

Using a Simple Manometer

A manometer can be used to measure pressure in the laboratory. A manometer consists of a U-shaped tube filled with a liquid (usually water or mercury). One end of the tube is connected to the chamber where the pressure is to be monitored, and the other end is open to the lab.

U-tube

The height difference of the liquid on either side of the tube (Δh) is directly proportional to the pressure difference between the chamber and the lab (ΔP). The pressure difference can be measured with a ruler and be recorded in units of mmHg or mmH$_2$O. Often the actual pressure of the lab (atmospheric pressure) can be measured with a barometer. Consult your instructor to find out whether a barometer is available to you. If you know the atmospheric pressure and ΔP, then the pressure of the gas in the chamber can be calculated using simple addition or subtraction.

If your manometer contains mercury, be careful. If the pressure in the chamber increases dramatically, there is a danger that the mercury could be ejected from the tube into the lab. (Note that most mercury manometers have a "safety trap" to prevent that from happening.)

Voltage Data Collection

The potential difference between two processes (for example, half–reactions) can be measured using a voltmeter. One wire from the voltmeter is attached to one half–reaction, another wire from the voltmeter is attached to the other half–reaction, and the voltage is read on a digital or other type readout. Voltmeters typically do not require calibration prior to taking measurements. Voltmeters are inexpensive and readily available. A CBL or MBL equipped with a voltage probe can function as a voltmeter.

Voltmeter

Familiarize yourself with the voltmeter before taking measurements. Make sure you are measuring voltage and not some other property. Many voltmeters are capable of measuring resistance and current (amps) as well as voltage. Often you must select "voltage" or "volts" to specifically measure voltage. Consult your instructor or the operator's manual if you are not clear about how to measure voltage with your voltmeter.

Voltage Measurements with a Voltage Probe

To use the voltage probe, follow the same procedure for using the temperature probe except identify the "voltage" probe type. Like the temperature probe, the voltage probe may already calibrated so a calibration menu will probably not appear. After selecting the voltage probe, you can collect voltage data using the data collection mode appropriate for your experiment.

Vernier Voltage Probe
Photograph Courtesy of
Vernier Software & Technology

If a negative voltage reading is observed, then it can be made positive by reversing the leads. You should get the same numerical value, but positive. You should also note that when the voltage probe is not connected to anything, a default voltage reading of 2.0 V may be displayed with the CBL system.

Selected Laboratory Techniques

This appendix describes techniques commonly used in the chemistry laboratory. Included are the proper ways to use a balance, a pipet, a buret, a graduated cylinder, a Bunsen burner, filtration equipment, and a centrifuge. There is also information about titrations, graphing, and data processing.

Taking Mass Measurements

One very important rule to follow when taking mass measurements is **never put chemicals directly on the balance pan.** This can damage the balance. Always use weighing paper when measuring the mass of a solid, and of course, pour liquids into a preweighed container before measuring their mass.

Mass measurements are usually taken using either a triple beam balance or an electronic balance. The electronic balance has several advantages over the triple beam balance, but is significantly more expensive. If your balance is not like those described here, consult your instructor for directions on the proper use of your balance.

Triple Beam or Platform Balance

Zero the balance by adjusting the knob at one end of the balance. The adjustment knob is usually just a small weight that can be moved along a screwlike shaft. Check the zero point periodically since foreign matter may accumulate on the platform or on the beams and cause a slight change in the zero position.

After the balance has been zeroed, place the sample on the platform (remember to use weighing paper or an appropriate container) and move the large weight to the notch **just before** the notch which causes the pointer to drop. Then move the next weight to the right in the same fashion. Finally slide the small weight along the scale until the pointer rests at zero. The mass is the sum of all of the weight positions, read directly from the three beams.

Triple Beam Balance

Reading the Weight on a Triple Beam Balance

Electronic Balance

You should check to see that the balance is level before use. The balance should have a "leveling bubble." Adjust the length of each leg of the balance until the "leveling bubble" is in the center of its circular chamber.

An electronic balance is typically very easy to use. Simply turn the balance on and "tare." Taring the balance means zeroing the balance. After pushing the tare button, the balance should read 0.000 g. The last digit may fluctuate because of air currents in the room. This is expected. After taring the balance, place the sample on the pan (remember to use weighing paper or an appropriate container) and then read the mass directly from the balance display. It's very easy. Turn the balance off when finished.

Electronic Balance

The tare button can be used to measure the mass of a solid or liquid directly. Just place the weighing paper (or container) on the balance and tare. The paper (or container) now will read as 0.000 g. Then remove the paper (or container), place the desired solid (or liquid) into it, and return it to the balance pan. The mass shown on the balance display is now the mass of the solid (or liquid). **Never pour a liquid into a container while it is on the balance.**

Measuring Volume

Volume measurements are typically made with a graduated cylinder, pipet, buret, or volumetric flask. A beaker or Erlenmeyer flask can be used if accuracy is not important. Some volumetric devices are designed to accurately measure the volume of liquid **contained** and some devices are designed to accurately measure the volume of liquid **delivered** by it. A device marked with "TD" is designed to measure the amount delivered and a device marked with "TC" is designed to measure the volume of liquid contained. This section will describe the proper use of a graduated cylinder, pipet, buret, and volumetric flask.

Note that it is important to report your volume measurements with the correct number of significant figures. The number of significant figures varies with the type of equipment.

Graduated Cylinder

When reading the volume using a graduated cylinder, always read the bottom of the meniscus. Estimate one digit between the nearest two graduations. For example, if your graduated cylinder is marked with 1 mL graduations, and the bottom of your meniscus is between the 16 mL

Meniscus

and 17 mL marks, and you estimate it's $^3/_{10}$ of the way between 16 and 17, then you must report the volume as 16.3 mL.

Correct viewpoint

Reading a Meniscus

Pipet

A volumetric pipet is designed to **deliver** an accurate volume of liquid. Some pipets have graduations and some have only one line for measuring volume. It takes practice to use a pipet properly. Allow time for practice whenever carrying out an investigation that involves the use of a pipet.

If your pipet has graduations, then you can accurately measure the volume of liquid delivered by the pipet by taking a measurement before and one after your delivery, and reporting the difference as the volume delivered. The number of significant figures will depend on the markings. You should always estimate one digit as with the graduated cylinder (discussed earlier).

If your pipet has only one line for measuring volume, then this line represents a volume delivery accurate to four significant figures. For example, if a 25 mL pipet is filled so that the bottom of the meniscus is just touching that line, then 25.00 mL of volume will be delivered upon draining that pipet. Note that a pipet is not really emptied when used properly.

To use a pipet,

1. Use a bulb to draw the liquid to a level above the desired amount (above the mark). **Never draw a liquid by sucking the end of the pipet.**

2. Remove the bulb and quickly place your index finger over the end of the pipet. By adjusting your finger pressure, allow the liquid to drain to the line. Sometimes you can slow the flow of the liquid by touching the pipet tip to the bottom of the container.

3. Remove the pipet from the solution (keeping your finger pressure on the end) and remove any lingering drops from the tip by touching the tip to the side of the container. Wipe off any liquid on the outside of the pipet with a paper towel.

4. To deliver the liquid, remove your finger from the pipet end. After draining, touch the tip to the side of the receiving vessel. You have now delivered a volume accurate to four significant figures.

You may notice there is still some liquid in the pipet tip. That's okay. If you use a bulb to "blow" that extra liquid into the receiving vessel, then you will deliver too much liquid.

Using a Pipet

Buret

A buret is designed to deliver a volume accurate to ± 0.01 mL. The buret should be secured in a proper buret stand when in use. A delivered volume is measured by simply taking a reading from the bottom of the meniscus before and after the delivery. The difference in readings is the volume delivered. The delivery is accomplished by opening the stopcock at the bottom of the buret. The flow rate can be controlled by adjusting the stopcock position. Most laboratory burets hold 50 mL and are marked in tenths of a mL.

A buret in a proper stand

*Meniscus
in a buret*

Using a stopcock

You should always rinse your buret with a few portions of the solution prior to filling. It is good practice to use a funnel when filling the buret, and to hold the buret below eye level when filling. It is important to remove all air bubbles from the buret tip before using the buret to make measurements. This is usually accomplished by allowing the liquid to flow through the tip until all of the air bubbles are blown out.

Volumetric Flask

A volumetric flask is designed to contain an accurate volume of liquid. It is normally used to prepare a solution where a final volume measurement is needed. A volumetric flask has one volume mark on the neck of the flask. A typical volumetric flask is assumed to be accurate to four significant figures. For example, if a 50 mL volumetric flask is filled to the mark, then it contains 50.00 mL.

250 mL
volumetric flask   0.435g KMnO₄

The KMnO₄ is first dissolved in a small amount of water.

Distilled water is added to fill the flask with solution just to the mark on the flask.

A mark on the neck of a volumetric flask indicates a volume of exactly 250 mL at 25 8C.

To use a volumetric flask,

1. Select the volume desired. Volumetric flasks come in many volumes. The most common are 10, 25, 50, 100, 250, 500, and 1000 mL.

2. Place a measured amount of solute, or solution to be diluted, into the clean volumetric flask.

3. Add deionized water to the flask until it is about ¾ filled, and dissolve the solute by swirling.

4. Add more water until the meniscus gets close to the mark on the neck of the flask. Then add water drop by drop until the bottom of the meniscus just touches the mark.

5. Stopper and invert the flask several times to ensure complete mixing. You have now prepared a solution with a volume measurement accurate to four significant figures.

Using a Bunsen Burner

A Bunsen burner produces a flame for heating things in the laboratory. The burner must be connected to a source of natural gas (methane). The burner will typically have a valve to control the gas flow rate. Most also have an airflow control. The gas and air are mixed in the Bunsen burner and ignited to produce the desired flame.

To light the burner, adjust the air control so that a minimum of air is supplied, turn on the gas, and hold a lighted match (or other lighter) above and to one side of the gas flow. After ignition, increase the airflow until a blue flame is obtained. The hottest part of the flame is just above the inner blue cone of the flame. If the blue cone is absent, increase the air flow. If the flame rises above the burner, turn down the gas flow. If the flame blows out, turn down the air flow. Never leave a flaming Bunsen burner unattended.

When heating a glass vessel such as a test tube, make sure you are using Pyrex or Kimax glassware, which can withstand the intense heat. When heating a test tube, always use a test tube holder and don't point the opening of the test tube at anyone. When heating other vessels, use a ring stand, ring, and wire gauze to hold the vessel above the burner.

Proper use of a Bunsen burner

Filtration (Separating a Solid and a Liquid)

A solid and a liquid can be separated using filtration or centrifugation. This section describes the techniques of filtration.

Gravity Filtration

1. Fold a circular piece of filter paper in half. Fold in half again.
2. Open the paper to form a cone and fit the cone into a funnel.
3. Wet the paper with a few milliliters of deionized water (or other appropriate solvent) and press the cone to the sides of the funnel so it fits tightly.
4. Pour the mixture into the cone. A clear solution should come through the filter and run through the funnel into a clean container.

Filter Paper

Gravity filtration

Avoid filling the filter too full. It is desirable to have the stem of the funnel on the side of the receiving container so the liquid filtrate doesn't splatter. Make sure the funnel stem is not submerged in liquid. This could prevent the flow of liquid through the filter.

Suction Filtration

1. Place a piece of filter paper flat against a Büchner funnel bottom and moisten with deionized water (or other appropriate solvent) to seal.
2. Place the funnel onto a side-arm flask with an appropriate vacuum seal.
3. Attach a vacuum line. A vacuum can be created by flowing water from a faucet through an aspirator.
4. Turn on the vacuum (or aspirator).
5. Pour the mixture into the Büchner funnel. The solution should be pulled through the funnel.

Suction filtration apparatus

6. The solid residue should be washed with deionized water. If deionized water could re-dissolve the solid, then wash it with another solvent. If the liquid filtrate is to be kept, then don't wash the solid residue until after the filtrate has been removed from the side-arm flask.
7. The solid can be dried by allowing air to be pulled through it by the vacuum.
8. Make sure to disconnect the apparatus before you turn off the vacuum or aspirator. Otherwise, if you are using an aspirator, you could potentially draw tap water from the aspirator into your flask.

Using a Centrifuge

A centrifuge is a device used to separate a solid from a liquid by centrifugal force. It usually consists of four to eight openings in a rotor head. The rotor head spins at high speed, causing the usually more dense solid to be driven to the bottom of the test tube containing the mixture. The liquid can then be removed by decanting (pouring) or by withdrawing with a capillary pipet.

Centrifuge

To use a centrifuge:

1. Place the sample to be separated into a test tube that will fit into the rotor head openings.
2. Pour deionized water into another test tube (same size) to the same depth as the mixture in the sample tube. This tube will act as a counterweight to keep the centrifuge balanced.
3. Place the test tubes into the rotor openings opposite one another.
4. Turn on the centrifuge and allow it to attain full speed.
5. Allow the centrifuge to run. Some mixtures separate in about one minute. Others can take up to eight minutes.
6. Switch off the centrifuge and allow it to stop without assistance. It's dangerous to touch the rotor while it's spinning.
7. Remove both test tubes.
8. If the solid is separated from the liquid, pour the liquid out (this is called decanting). You could also draw out the liquid with a disposable pipet. The liquid solution should be free of solid particles.
9. The solid is still contaminated with the solution and should be washed. Add a few mL of deionized water to the solid and mix well. Centrifuge and decant.

Centrifuged samples of two different solids

10. Repeat step 9 two more times. Your solid should now be free of contamination from the dissolved ions.

Titration

A titration is used to determine the concentration of a solution by reacting it with a measured amount of another solution of known concentration. The solution of known concentration is called the **standard solution.** A carefully measured volume of one solution is placed in an Erlenmeyer flask along with a few drops of an indicator solution. The other solution is slowly added from a buret into the swirling Erlenmeyer flask until the stoichiometric equivalence point is reached. This is observed by a change in color of the indicator. It is also possible to detect an equivalence point using a pH meter or other device.

Once the two solution volumes are known, the concentration of the solution can be calculated using these volumes and the concentration of the standard solution. For example, if 25.00 mL of H_2SO_4 (aq) (unknown concentration) were pipeted into an Erlenmeyer flask, and 22.08 mL of 0.1035 M NaOH (aq) were added to reach the equivalence point, then the H_2SO_4 (aq) concentration can be calculated as follows:

First calculate the number of moles of NaOH delivered during the titration:

$$\frac{0.1035 \text{ mol NaOH}}{1 \text{ L NaOH (aq)}} \times [0.02208 \text{ L NaOH (aq)}] = 2.285 \times 10^{-3} \text{ mol NaOH}$$

Then, using the balanced equation, calculate the number of moles of H_2SO_4 that must have reacted with the added NaOH:

$$2 \text{ NaOH (aq)} + H_2SO_4 \text{ (aq)} \rightarrow 2 H_2O \text{ (l)} + Na_2SO_4 \text{ (aq)}$$

$$[2.285 \times 10^{-3} \text{ mol NaOH}] \times \frac{1 \text{ mol } H_2SO_4}{2 \text{ mol NaOH}} = 1.143 \times 10^{-3} \text{ mol } H_2SO_4$$

Finally, determine the mole/L ratio for the H_2SO_4 solution knowing the moles of H_2SO_4 that reacted and the volume of H_2SO_4 (aq) used:

$$\frac{1.143 \times 10^{-3} \text{ mol } H_2SO_4}{0.02500 \text{ L } H_2SO_4 \text{ (aq)}} = 0.04571 \ M \ H_2SO_4$$

The final step of your calculation may be to determine the grams of acid consumed, or some other quantity; but the theme is always the same. A reaction is carried out to its stoichiometric equivalence point, and the moles of solute that reacted from a solution is determined by knowing the moles of solute that reacted from the standard solution, and knowing the mole:mole ratio in which the two substances react.

Graphing and Data Processing

Data tables and graphs are used in scientific reports because they can convey a great deal of information about an experiment in a concise fashion. This section will give some general guidelines about reporting data and graphing, and will point out the numerous advantages of computer-aided graphing.

Guidelines:

1. Graphs and tables should always have an appropriate title.
2. Graphs and tables should always clearly report the units for each numerical entry. On a graph, the axes should be labeled with the appropriate variable name, and the units. Table entries should contain units, or should have the units clearly shown in the table heading.
3. If a table entry is a calculated value, then the calculation should be shown as a footnote to the table. For example, if the mass of a container is in row 1, and the mass of the container with solid is in row 2, and the mass of the solid is in row 3, and the mass of the solid was found from the other two values, then an appropriate footnote to the table would be:

$$\text{mass solid} = (\text{mass container with solid}) - (\text{mass container})$$

4. Graphs should be large enough to show any trends in the data. It is usually preferable for the graph to be scaled so that the data fill the entire graphing area, and for the graph to fill an entire page.

Graphing

Graphs can be generated by hand using graph paper, or by using a computer equipped with graphing software such as Graphical Analysis, Excel, CricketGraph, or any other similar software. When using a computer, many of the steps required for producing a good graph are done automatically.

Graphing by Hand

When graphing by hand, it is important to scale the x and y axes such that all of the data are included and they fill the graphing area. For example, if the x values range from 0 to 56, then your x axis might range from 0 to 60. Similarly, if your y values range from 2×10^{-2} to 8.6×10^{-1}, then your y axis might range from 1×10^{-2} to 1.

Once your x and y axis ranges are determined, label the axes with their appropriate variable names and units. Enter x and y values at even intervals along the axes to show the range along each axis. Plot the points using a sharp pencil.

If the data show, or are supposed to show a linear trend, it would be appropriate to draw a straight line through the data points, and determine the slope and y intercept of the line. Often the data are not in a perfectly straight line, and you will need to draw the best straight line you can while considering all of the data points. The line may touch several points, but probably not all of them. Ask your instructor to help if you need to draw a straight line through data points that are not in a straight line. Once the line is drawn, you can calculate the slope by picking two convenient points **along the line** (not necessarily data points) and dividing the difference in y values by the difference in x values:

$$\text{slope (m)} = \frac{(y_1 - y_2)}{(x_1 - x_2)}$$

This calculation may give a negative number, corresponding to a declining slope; or a positive number, corresponding to a rising slope. The y intercept is determined by observing where the line crosses the y axis. This is the y value when x = 0. You can also determine the y intercept value mathematically using the equation of the line:

$$y = mx + b$$

If you have a y value, its corresponding x value, and the slope of the line (m), you can solve the equation for the y intercept (b).

Graphing with a Computer

To graph with a computer, the data must be imported (or typed) into a graphing software program such as Graphical Analysis. The Graphical Analysis software allows direct importing of data from a graphing calculator (under the File menu). Once your data is stored on the computer, it can probably (depending on the age and model of your computer) be simply highlighted and cut and then pasted into the graphing program of your choice.

The graphing program will show your imported (or typed) data in columns. At some point you will need to assign labels for each column of data.

Graphing is often as simple as pushing a button and choosing which variable you want on the x axis and which variable you want plotted on the y-axis. You can also choose to plot multiple data sets on the same graph. After making your choices, the graph will appear automatically scaled. At this point you can usually assign a title, edit the axis labels, adjust the scale, put in gridlines, ask the computer to draw the best straight line fit and report the slope and intercept, view the graph as it would look on a page when printed, or just about anything else you could imagine to help you create a professional–quality graph.

The exact steps you take to polish your graph will vary from program to program. Familiarize yourself with the graphing program available to you and take advantage of its tremendous capability.

If you need to do a mathematical operation on your data, then graphing and spreadsheet programs easily allow you to write a formula in another column that carries out the calculation. Suppose you have a column of Celsius temperature data that you want to convert to Fahrenheit. Your software is probably capable of accepting the mathematical formula for converting the data. The software will then automatically convert the entire column into the converted values, and display the converted data in a new column. This is a very valuable tool for laboratory investigations. You should know how to convert and/or manipulate columns of data using the graphing software available to you.

Laboratory Equipment

1 – beaker	18 – spatula
2 – Büchner funnel	19 – spot plate
3 – Bunsen burner	20 – stirring rod
4 – buret	21 – support ring
5 – clay triangle	22 – test tube
6 – crucible and lid	23 – test tube brush
7 – crucible tongs	24 – test tube holder
8 – Erlenmeyer flask	25 – test tube rack
9 – evaporating dish	26 – thermometer
10 – eye dropper	27 – transfer pipet
11 – filter flask	28 – utility clamp
12 – Florence flask	29 – volumetric flask
13 – funnel	30 – wash bottle
14 – graduated cylinder	31 – watch glass
15 – measuring pipet	32 – wide mouth bottle
16 – pinch clamp	33 – wing top
17 – pipet bulb	34 – wire gauze

Sample Material Safety Data Sheet

Acetone
00140

**** SECTION 1 - CHEMICAL PRODUCT AND COMPANY IDENTIFICATION ****

MSDS Name: Acetone
Synonyms:
   Dimethylformaldehyde, dimethyl ketone, 2-propanone, pyroacetic acid, pyroacetic ether
Company Identification:

For information, call:
Emergency Number:
For CHEMTREC assistance, call:

**** SECTION 2 - COMPOSITION, INFORMATION ON INGREDIENTS ****

CAS#	Chemical Name	%	EINECS#
67-64-1	2-propanone	99	200-662-2

**** SECTION 3 - HAZARDS IDENTIFICATION ****

EMERGENCY OVERVIEW

Appearance: Colorless, highly volatile liquid. Flash Point: -4°F. Danger! Extremely flammable liquid. May cause central nervous system depression. May cause liver and kidney damage. Causes eye and skin irritation. Causes digestive and respiratory tract irritation. Target Organs: Kidneys, central nervous system, liver, respiratory system.

Potential Health Effects
  Eye:
      Produces irritation, characterized by a burning sensation, redness, tearing, inflammation, and possible corneal injury.
  Skin:
      Exposure may cause irritation characterized by redness, dryness, and inflammation.
  Ingestion:
      May cause irritation of the digestive tract. May cause central nervous system depression, kidney damage, and liver damage. Symptoms may include: headache, excitement, fatigue, nausea, vomiting, stupor, and coma.
  Inhalation:
      Inhalation of high concentrations may cause central nervous system effects characterized by headache, dizziness, unconsciousness and coma. Causes respiratory tract irritation. May cause liver and kidney damage. May cause motor incoordination and speech abnormalities.
  Chronic:
      Prolonged or repeated skin contact may cause dermatitis. Chronic inhalation may cause effects similar to those of acute inhalation.

Source: Fisher Scientific MSDS Web site, http://www.fisher1.com.

**** SECTION 4 - FIRST AID MEASURES ****

Eyes:
    Flush eyes with plenty of water for at least 15 minutes, occasionally lifting the upper and lower lids. Get
    medical aid immediately.
Skin:
    Flush skin with plenty of soap and water for at least 15 minutes while removing contaminated clothing and
    shoes. Get medical aid if irritation develops or persists.
Ingestion:
    If victim is conscious and alert, give 2-4 cupfuls of milk or water. Get medical aid immediately.
Inhalation:
    Get medical aid immediately. Remove from exposure to fresh air immediately. If not breathing, give
    artificial respiration. If breathing is difficult, give oxygen.
Notes to Physician:
    Treat symptomatically and supportively.
    No specific antidote exists.

**** SECTION 5 - FIRE FIGHTING MEASURES ****

General Information:
    Containers can build up pressure if exposed to heat and/or fire. As in any fire, wear a self-contained
    breathing apparatus in pressure-demand, MSHA/NIOSH (approved or equivalent), and full protective gear.
    Vapors can travel to a source of ignition and flash back. Use water spray to keep fire-exposed containers
    cool.
Extinguishing Media:
    For small fires, use dry chemical, carbon dioxide, water spray or alcohol-resistant foam. For large fires, use
    water spray, fog, or alcohol-resistant foam.
Autoignition Temperature: 33°F (0.56°C)
Flash Point: -4°F (-17.78°C)
NFPA Rating: health-1; flammability-3; reactivity-0
Explosion Limits, Lower: 2.5
            Upper: 12.8

**** SECTION 6 - ACCIDENTAL RELEASE MEASURES ****

General Information: Use proper personal protective equipment as indicated in Section 8.
Spills/Leaks:
    Absorb spill with inert material, (e.g., dry sand or earth), then place into a chemical waste container. Wear
    appropriate protective clothing to minimize contact with skin. Remove all sources of ignition.

**** SECTION 7 - HANDLING and STORAGE ****

Handling:
    Wash thoroughly after handling. Remove contaminated clothing and wash before reuse. Use with adequate
    ventilation. Avoid contact with eyes, skin, and clothing. Empty containers retain product residue, (liquid
    and/or vapor), and can be dangerous. Do not pressurize, cut, weld, braze, solder, drill, grind, or expose such
    containers to heat, sparks or open flames.
Storage:
    Keep away from sources of ignition. Store in a tightly closed container.

**** SECTION 8 - EXPOSURE CONTROLS, PERSONAL PROTECTION ****

Engineering Controls:

Use process enclosure, local exhaust ventilation, or other engineering controls to control airborne levels below recommended exposure limits.

Exposure Limits

Chemical Name	ACGIH	NIOSH	OSHA - Final PELs
2-propanone	750 ppm; 1780 mg/m3; 1000 ppm STEL; 2380 mg/m3 STEL	250 ppm TWA; 590 mg/m3 TWA	1000 ppm TWA; 2400 mg/m3 TWA

OSHA Vacated PELs:

2-propanone:

750 ppm TWA; 1800 mg/m3 TWA; 1000 ppm STEL; 2400 mg/m3 STEL

Personal Protective Equipment

Eyes:

Wear chemical goggles and face shield.

Skin:

Wear appropriate gloves to prevent skin exposure.

Clothing:

Wear polyethylene gloves, apron, and/or clothing.

Respirators:

Follow the OSHA respirator regulations found in 29CFR 1910.134. Always use a NIOSH-approved respirator when necessary.

**** SECTION 9 - PHYSICAL AND CHEMICAL PROPERTIES ****

Physical State:	Liquid
Appearance:	Colorless, highly volatile liquid.
Odor:	Sweetish.
pH:	7
Vapor Pressure:	180 mm Hg
Vapor Density:	2.0 (Air=1)
Evaporation Rate:	7.7 (n-Butyl acetate=1)
Viscosity:	Not available
Boiling Point:	133.2°F
Freezing/Melting Point:	-139.6°F
Decomposition Temperature:	Not available.
Solubility:	Not available.
Specific Gravity/Density:	0.79 (Water=1)
Molecular Formula:	C3H6O
Molecular Weight:	58.0414

**** SECTION 10 - STABILITY AND REACTIVITY ****

Chemical Stability:
   Stable.
Conditions to Avoid:
   High temperatures, temperatures above 220°C.
Incompatibilities with Other Materials:
   Forms explosive mixtures with hydrogen peroxide, acetic acid, nitric acid, nitric acid+sulfuric acid, chromic anhydride, chromyl chloride, nitrosyl chloride, hexachloromelamine, nitrosyl perchlorate, nitryl perchlorate, permonosulfuric acid, thiodiglycol+hydrogen peroxide.
Hazardous Decomposition Products:
   Carbon monoxide, carbon dioxide.
Hazardous Polymerization: Has not been reported.

**** SECTION 11 - TOXICOLOGICAL INFORMATION ****

RTECS#:
   CAS# 67-64-1: AL3150000
LD50/LC50:
   CAS# 67-64-1: Inhalation, rat: LC50 =50100 mg/m3/8H; Oral, mouse: LD50 = 3 gm/kg; Oral, rabbit: LD50 = 5340 mg/kg; Oral, rat: LD50 = 5800 mg/kg; Skin, rabbit: LD50 = 20 gm/kg.
Carcinogenicity:
   2-propanone -
   Not listed by ACGIH, IARC, NIOSH, NTP, or OSHA.
Epidemiology:
   No information available.
Teratogenicity:
   No information available.
Reproductive Effects:
   Fertility: post-implantation mortality. Ihl, mam: TCLo=31500 ug/m3/24H (1-13D preg)
Neurotoxicity:
   No information available.
Mutagenicity:
   Cytogenetic analysis: hamster fibroblast, 40 g/L Sex chromosome loss/non-disjunction: S.cerevisiae, 47600 ppm
Other Studies:
   None.

**** SECTION 12 - ECOLOGICAL INFORMATION ****

Ecotoxicity:
   Rainbow trout LC50=5540 mg/L/96H Sunfish (tap water), death at 14250 ppm/24H Mosquito fish (turbid water) TLm=13000 ppm/48H
Environmental Fate:
   Volatilizes, leeches, and biodegrades when released to soil.
Physical/Chemical:
   No information available.
Other:
   None.

**** SECTION 13 - DISPOSAL CONSIDERATIONS ****

Dispose of in a manner consistent with federal, state, and local regulations.
RCRA D-Series Maximum Concentration of Contaminants: Not listed.
RCRA D-Series Chronic Toxicity Reference Levels: Not listed.
RCRA F-Series: Not listed.
RCRA P-Series: Not listed.
RCRA U-Series: waste number U002 (Ignitable waste)
This material is banned from land disposal according to RCRA.

**** SECTION 14 - TRANSPORT INFORMATION ****

US DOT
    Shipping Name: ACETONE
    Hazard Class: 3
        UN Number: UN1090
    Packing Group: II
IMO
    Shipping Name: ACETONE
    Hazard Class: 3.1
        UN Number: 1090
    Packing Group: 2
IATA
    Shipping Name: ACETONE
    Hazard Class: 3
        UN Number: 1090
    Packing Group: 2
RID/ADR
    Shipping Name: ACETONE
Dangerous Goods Code: 3(3B)
        UN Number: 1090
Canadian TDG
    Shipping Name: ACETONE
    Hazard Class: 3
        UN Number: UN1090
    Other Information: FLASHPOINT -20 C

**** SECTION 15 - REGULATORY INFORMATION ****

A. Federal
  TSCA
    CAS# 67-64-1 is listed on the TSCA inventory.
    Health & Safety Reporting List
      None of the chemicals are on the Health & Safety Reporting List.
    Chemical Test Rules
      None of the chemicals in this product are under a Chemical Test Rule.
    Section 12b
      None of the chemicals are listed under TSCA Section 12b.
    TSCA Significant New Use Rule
      None of the chemicals in this material have a SNUR under TSCA.
  SARA
    Section 302 (RQ)
      None of the chemicals in this material have an RQ.

Section 302 (TPQ)
None of the chemicals in this product have a TPQ.
SARA Codes
CAS # 67-64-1: acute, chronic, flammable, sudden release of pressure.
Section 313
This chemical is not at a high enough concentration to be reportable under Section 313.
No chemicals are reportable under Section 313.
Clean Air Act:
This material does not contain any hazardous air pollutants.
This material does not contain any Class 1 Ozone depletors.
This material does not contain any Class 2 Ozone depletors.
Clean Water Act:
None of the chemicals in this product are listed as Hazardous Substances under the CWA.
None of the chemicals in this product are listed as Priority Pollutants under the CWA.
None of the chemicals in this product are listed as Toxic Pollutants under the CWA.
OSHA:
None of the chemicals in this product are considered highly hazardous by OSHA.
B. State
2-propanone can be found on the following state right to know lists: California, New Jersey, Florida, Pennsylvania, Minnesota, Massachusetts.
California No Significant Risk Level:
None of the chemicals in this product are listed.
MSDS Creation Date: 11/30/1994 Revision Date: 8/13/1996

The information above is believed to be accurate and represents the best information currently available to us. However, we make no warranty of merchantability or any other warranty, express or implied, with respect to such information, and we assume no liability resulting from its use. Users should make their own investigations to determine the suitability of the information for their particular purposes. In no way shall Fisher be liable for any claims, losses, or damages of any third party or for lost profits or any special, indirect, incidental, consequential or exemplary damages, howsoever arising, even if Fisher has been advised of the possibility of such damages.

Tables

Vapor Pressure of Liquid Water at Various Temperatures

Temperature ($^\circ$C)	Vapor Pressure (torr)	Temperature ($^\circ$C)	Vapor Pressure (torr)
10.0	9.209	26.0	25.209
12.0	10.518	27.0	26.739
13.0	11.231	28.0	28.349
14.0	11.987	29.0	30.043
15.0	12.788	30.0	31.824
16.0	13.634	31.0	33.695
17.0	14.530	32.0	35.663
18.0	15.477	33.0	37.729
19.0	16.477	34.0	39.898
20.0	17.535	35.0	42.175
21.0	18.650	40.0	55.324
22.0	19.827	45.0	71.88
23.0	21.068	50.0	92.51
24.0	22.377	55.0	118.04
25.0	23.756	60.0	149.38

Density of Water at Various Temperatures

Temperature ($^\circ$C)	Density (g/mL)	Temperature ($^\circ$C)	Density (g/mL)
10.0	0.9997026	26.0	0.9967867
12.0	0.9995004	27.0	0.9965162
13.0	0.9993801	28.0	0.9962365
14.0	0.9992474	29.0	0.9959478
15.0	0.9991026	30.0	0.9956502
16.0	0.9989460	31.0	0.9953440
17.0	0.9987779	32.0	0.9950292
18.0	0.9985986	33.0	0.9947060
19.0	0.9984082	34.0	0.9943745
20.0	0.9982071	35.0	0.9940349
21.0	0.9979955	40.0	0.9922187
22.0	0.9977735	45.0	0.9902162
23.0	0.9975415	50.0	0.9880393
24.0	0.9972995	55.0	0.9856982
25.0	0.9970479	60.0	0.9832018

Molarities of Concentrated Acids and Bases

Solution	Concentration
Ammonia, NH_3	15 M
Hydrochloric Acid, HCl	12 M
Nitric Acid, HNO_3	16 M
Sulfuric Acid, H_2SO_4	18 M
Phosphoric Acid, H_3PO_4	18 M

Solubility Rules for Ionic Compounds

Substance	Rules
Na^+, K^+, NH_4^+, NO_3^-	Ionic compounds which contain these ions are soluble.
SO_4^{2-}	Most ionic compounds containing sulfate are soluble. Exceptions are: $BaSO_4$, $SrSO_4$, $PbSO_4$, $CaSO_4$, Hg_2SO_4, and Ag_2SO_4 (partially soluble).
Cl^-, Br^-, I^-	Most compounds containing chloride, bromide, or iodide are soluble. Exceptions are: AgX, Hg_2X_2, PbX_2, $HgBr_2$, and HgI_2. $PbCl_2$ is somewhat insoluble.
Ag^+	Ionic compounds containing Ag^+ are insoluble except $AgNO_3$.
OH^-	Most ionic hydroxide compounds are insoluble. Exceptions are: $NaOH$, KOH, $NH_3(aq)$, $Ba(OH)_2$ (somewhat insoluble), and $Ca(OH)_2$ (partially soluble).
S^{2-}	Most ionic sulfide compounds are insoluble. Exceptions are: Group IA, Group IIA, and NH_4^+ sulfides.
CrO_4^{2-}	Most ionic chromate compounds are insoluble. Exceptions are: K^+, Na^+, NH_4^+, Mg^+, Ca^{2+}, Al^{3+}, and Ni^{2+}.
CO_3^{2-}, PO_4^{3-}, SO_3^{2-}, SiO_3^{2-}	Most ionic carbonate, phosphate, sulfite, and silicate compounds are insoluble. Exceptions are: K^+, Na^+, and NH_4^+ compounds.

